Photos for Building Language Skills

Strengthen Receptive and Expressive Language Skills, Use as an Alternative Communication System, or to Teach English

by
Sherrill B. Flora

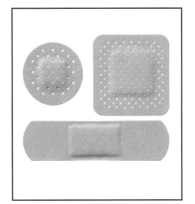

Publisher
Key Education Publishing Company, LLC
Minneapolis, Minnesota

CONGRATULATIONS ON YOUR PURCHASE OF A KEY EDUCATION PRODUCT!

The editors at Key Education are former teachers who bring experience, enthusiasm, and quality to each and every product. Thousands of teachers have looked to the staff at Key Education for new and innovative resources to make their work more enjoyable and rewarding. We are committed to developing and publishing educational materials that will assist teachers in building a strong and developmentally appropriate curriculum for young children.

PLAN FOR GREAT TEACHING EXPERIENCES WHEN YOU USE EDUCATIONAL MATERIALS FROM KEY EDUCATION PUBLISHING COMPANY, LLC

Credits
Author: Sherrill B. Flora
Creative Director: Annette Hollister-Papp
Editors: George C. Flora, Karen Seberg
Production: Key Education Staff
Photo Credits: © Sherrill B. Flora, © Comstock, © Eyewire, © Shutterstock, © Hermera, © BananaStock, © Rubberball

Key Education welcomes manuscripts and product ideas from teachers. For a copy of our submission guidelines, please send a self-addressed, stamped envelope to:

**Key Education Publishing Company, LLC
Acquisitions Department
9601 Newton Avenue South
Minneapolis, Minnesota 55431**

Table of Contents

Introduction
"A picture is worth a thousand words!"

Photographs are incredibly effective visual teaching tools. They can be an open-ended resource that communicates information, helps children understand new concepts, gives meaning to vocabulary, or introduces new topics. Photographs can be used to teach basic skills, build language, and provide a visual tool in all curriculum subjects. Photographs provide opportunities for discussion, making comparisons, and for observing and describing details. Photographs can offer students a wealth of potential learning experiences.

Photos for Building Language Skills is a comprehensive collection of over 900 realistic photographs, organized by themes and topics *(see Table of Contents, pages 3–6)*. Speech and language pathologists, teachers in early childhood, elementary, special education, and English language development programs will quickly discover that *Photos for Building Language Skills* is an essential educational resource!

Directions for Preparing and Storing the Photographs

Here are the directions for removing the photographs from the book, preparing them for use, and storing them after use:

1. **Remove the photographs:** To remove a page, cut along the fold with an X-acto knife™ or sharp scissors. Cut out the individual photographs along the dashed lines and then laminate for durability.

2. **Words or no words:** Each photograph comes with the printed word. You may choose to leave the word attached to the photograph or cut off the word. Keeping the word attached to the photograph can encourage literacy skills. It may be possible for the student to eventually use only the printed words instead of photographs.

3. **Store the photos:** Organize and store the photographs by themes or alphabetically. Place the laminated photographs in file boxes with index tabs separating each section. Once the photographs are organized, the teacher or parent can easily pick and choose the cards they wish to incorporate into the student's vocabulary, games, lessons, calendars, or schedules.

Using Photographs in English Language Development Programs

English language development (ELD) teachers have known for years that photographs are an essential educational resource for English language learners (ELL)—especially those ELL students who are newcomers or have little or no understanding of the English language. In ELD programs, photographs can become a powerful communication medium that helps students make connections between new words and the meaning of those words.

Photographs can be used to:
- create a print-rich environment using photographs and print as classroom labels
- match new vocabulary to its visual image, as well as to teach grammar, pronunciation, and intonation in the context of a theme or topic
- provide understanding of basic concepts such as next to, between, over, under ... etc.
- can be used in a large variety of teacher-created learning games, such as:
  - memory match/concentration
  - lotto and bingo games (using thematic topics, parts of speech, special classroom topics... etc.)
  - sorting and classifying according to themes or parts of speech (noun, verb, adjective)
  - use two photographs as a springboard for comparing and contrasting similarities and differences
  - build receptive language skills by displaying 4 to 6 photos; describe one photo and then have students select the photo that was described
  - display photos on a bulletin board and place white speech bubbles above each photo, and then have students either write or dictate a caption or speech sentence for each photo

Using Photographs in Preschool and Kindergarten Classrooms

Although language begins before children even learn to talk, it is generally accepted that most children between the ages of 2 and 5 acquire most of their language, beginning with simple two-word phrases and eventually speaking in full complex sentences. Most children naturally learn how to use past, present, and future tenses, use singular and plurals, and are able to make statements, give information, and ask questions.

The differences in language acquisition at age 5, when many children are entering kindergarten, can be shocking. One child may begin kindergarten with a vocabulary of over 5000 words, while another child may have a more limited vocabulary of possibly less than 1000 words. It has been estimated that 10% of kindergartners have a significant speech and language problem. Helping young children increase their vocabulary is an important step to ensuring school success.

At the preschool and kindergarten level, photographs can be used:
- to describe the details of objects
- to sequence the events of the day
- as visual materials to create a print-rich environment
- as a catalyst for telling and retelling stories
- for sorting and classifying animals, people, objects, actions, etc.
- to teach basic skills and language concepts such as positional and directional words, opposites, shapes, colors, the alphabet, and numbers
- to increase listening, speaking, and comprehension skills

Using Photographs in the Elementary Classroom

Photographs can be used for the following purposes:
- to teach, practice, and review new vocabulary
- to teach and practice grammatical structures, such as: *Present tense:* What do you see? What is that? Who are they? *Present continuous:* What is happening? What are they doing? *Simple past:* What happened? Why do you think . . ? *Past continuous:* What were they doing? Where were they going?
- to provide speaking practice with discussions and problem-solving
- to use as picture prompts for writing experiences
- to explore history, science, and current social issues

Using Photographs with Students who have Communication Disorders/Special Education Needs

According to the National Dissemination Center for Children with Disabilities (NICHCY), communication disorders affect 1 in 10 people, and more than one million school age children, and approximately another 500,000 preschool children receive speech and language services. Several other studies suggest that 8 to 12 people per 1,000 experience severe communication impairments.

Speech and language pathologists have used photographs as visual tools to assist in correcting simple articulation errors (for example, an *S* and *Z* lisp and problems with *TH)*, problems with phonological disorders (where children struggle with how sounds are put together to form words), to the most significant communication deficits, including autism spectrum disorder (ASD, with as many as 50% being nonverbal), developmental delays, Down's syndrome, dyspraxia, and dysphasia (where the individual does not have the motor skills to support sign language).

One problem associated with severe speech and language problems is that the student may be nonverbal, have minimal speech, use meaningless or repetitive (echolalia) speech, or may lack the ability to engage in meaningful conversation. Often these students will need to be taught an alternative for verbal communication.

Augmentative and alternative communication (AAC) refers to ways in which a student can communicate without using speech. AAC techniques can include facial expressions, gestures, sign language, or visual aids such as photographs, pictures, drawings, symbols, letters, or words. There are even electronic devices that can actually speak for the student. Using AAC does not mean that the student will never acquire speech. Often, AAC will help to develop and encourage speech. The goal of AAC is to provide the most effective means of communication for each individual student.

AAC has three specific uses:
1. **Transitional AAC:** Many young children (very often children with Down's syndrome and ASD) who are not yet talking, are taught to use sign language (see page 185) or communication boards (see page 9) while they are learning speech. Transitional AAC allows children to communicate with others, increases receptive language, and lowers frustration levels.

2. **Supplemental AAC:** Students who are speaking, but have intelligibility problems, often benefit from AAC. It allows them to use speech and still use other means to help people understand what they are trying to communicate.

3. **Alternative AAC:** When a student is unable to use speech, AAC systems can serve as the student's primary means of communication. These are complicated systems that are designed to meet all the communication needs of the student.

Students with autism spectrum disorder (ASD) show impairments in imaginative play, social interactions, as well as communication skills. Not all, but a large majority of ASD students think visually, which explains why photographs can be such an effective communication tool. Temple Grandin provides an excellent description of how many people with ASD think and how it affects their ability to communicate. She wrote in her book, *Thinking in Pictures* (1996):

> *"I think in pictures. Words are like a second language to me. I translate both spoken and written words into full color movies, complete with sound, which run like a VCR tape in my head. When someone speaks to me, his words are instantly translated into pictures."*

This explanation provides evidence of why photographs can help the ASD student to communicate. Photographs or pictures placed on a communication board, in a communication binder, or used on calendars, schedules, or as household, furniture, and schoolroom labels allows a student to:

- indicate choices
- answer questions
- organize and navigate their environment
- develop a better understanding of expectations
- anticipate daily routines and events
- learn to communicate more effectively

Creating Calendars and Schedules

Calendars and schedules can help students with ASD to better understand what will happen next, make transitions easier, develop the concept of time, provide preparation for new experiences, decrease anxiety, and provide the student with a sense of security.

The Calendar (page 237): The calendar may be enlarged and reproduced for individual use. On the calendar fill in the month and number each day. Attach photographs to the calendar with self-stick Velcro®. Photographs from Chapter 10: Holidays and Seasons (pages 113–119) are essential for this activity. Photographs from Chapter 14: Nature & Weather (pages 135–141), such as sun, rain, and windy also work well. Photographs from Chapter 17: Places (pages 161–169) allow you to add special events and appointments, such as going to the beach or a dental appointment. Photographs for special activities can be added from Chapter 1: Actions/Verbs (pages 11–31) such as going shopping, painting, or camping.

Daily Home and School Schedules (pages 229–237): These pages may also be reproduced for individual use. Laminate for durability. Attach photos with self-stick Velcro®. *(See examples to the right.)*

Communication Boards, Binders, and Other Extra Fun Ideas Using Photographs

Any of the following visual communication tools offers the student a way to communicate that most people can easily understand. When utilizing any of the ideas below it is essential to choose vocabulary that will meet the specific needs, interests, and ability level of the student. A pictorial system of communicating requires constant updating and refreshing as the student's skills expand and their interests grow and change.

Here are some general guidelines for choosing vocabulary:
1. **Special interests and/or wants:** When students are first learning to use a pictorial system, the pictures/photos should have important meaning to the child or provide immediate gratification, such as getting something to eat or getting to play with a favorite toy.

2. **Labeling:** Labels for objects, people, places, feelings, or special activities—being able to communicate that he is happy/sad, doesn't feel well, can label everyday objects, can follow simple directions, is able to respond yes and no, and can make choices.

3. **Sharing information:** This is the beginning of conversation—being able to initiate and share information, is able to take-turns, respond to questions, and maintain a topic for a short period.

4. **Questioning:** Is able to ask questions—who, what, where, when, why, and how. This is an advanced communication skill that also involves the ability to ask for assistance or permission.

Communication boards: Any of the included charts and schedules (pages 229–237) can be used to create communication boards. Remove the pages from the book (pages may also be reproduced for individual use), laminate for durability, and attach the "hook" side of self-stick Velcro® in each section. Place the "loop" side of the self-stick Velcro® on the backs of the photos and then arrange them on the board. Communication boards can also be made from tag board, foam board, or you may use magnetic boards with self-stick magnetic tape placed only on the backs of the photographs.

Here are some examples of communication boards:

- **Food choices:** Many parents make communication boards that are hung on the refrigerator door. The photos on this board are of various foods that the child might request. If the student was asked what he would like to eat, the student would then point to, or take off, the photo of the food that he wanted. *(Food photos can also be placed on a refrigerator with self stick magnetic tape.)*

- **Activity choices:** This chart has photos of the student's daily routines or favorite activities, such as watching TV, coloring, playing a game, or going to the playground.

- **Favorite toy choices:** This chart has photos of favorite toys.

- **Reading faces/emotions:** This chart has photos of faces that represent a variety of emotions. Reading emotions in others is often difficult for many ASD students. Playing games and using a variety of visuals can be helpful in developing this skill.

- **Family/friends:** This chart has photos of family, friends, and people that the child sees often. It can be used to prepare the student for visitors or to review who they have recently seen. This can also be made for the staff at the student's school.

- **Home/school chores:** This chart has photos of "helping" activities, such as watering plants, setting the table, erasing the chalkboard, or picking up toys.

- **Clothing:** This chart has clothing photos, organized by the sequence of how a person gets dressed.

- **Topic boards:** These types of charts have a wide variety of uses. One chart could represent a visit to a doctor's office—the child would be able see ahead of time what might happen *(measuring height, weight, or a possible injection)*. Another example could be a toothbrushing chart—demonstrating visually each step of how to brush teeth. An animal chart could have photos of animals from the zoo, a farm, pets, or animals commonly viewed in the student's neighborhood.

Communication binders: Many different types of materials can be used to create communication binders. Photos can be organized in a photo album by theme, topic, or daily schedule, as well as in three-ring binders with sheet protectors or notebooks. Often a small-sized communication binder is effective and are easily made from small photo albums or pocket-size notebooks.

Extra fun ideas: Many students use a variety of communication materials, including photos that are glued on index cards, laminated, and held together with a brad, strung on a necklace, placed on a key chain, or even put in a special communication purse or wallet. Using fun materials can encourage students to want to use them.

Special Note About "Photos for Building Language Skills"

The photographs included in *Photos for Building Language Skills* are meant to be used as a supplement for AAC systems, in teaching games, in language lessons, and other visual classroom materials. They are not designed as a complete AAC system. AAC systems for a person with a severe communication disorder are complex and need the evaluations of the individual student's specialists and parents.

For teachers, therapists, and parents who are currently using an alternative picture system, the photographs in *Photos for Building Language Skills* can add a wealth of visual images to incorporate into an existing program.

Chapter 1: Actions/Verbs

The actions/verbs cards (pages 11 through 31) show actions from everyday life. Here are some ideas for encouraging expressive and receptive language skills:

1. Show the photo cards one at a time. Ask the student to describe what the child is doing in the picture.

2. Let the students pantomime the actions. One child pantomimes the action and the other children guess what the child is doing.

3. Place several cards in front of the student. Ask a question about one of the cards and have the student choose the correct card. "Which picture shows a child who is swimming?" "Which child is running?"

4. Play "What's missing?" Show the student several cards. Turn them upside down and then take one away. Show the cards again and ask which one is missing.

5. Play "Can you guess?" Ask a student to pick a card and not show anyone else. The student should describe some things about the card. The other students or family members guess the name of the action.

baking	**bathing**	**batting**

biking	**blowing bubbles**	**bouncing**

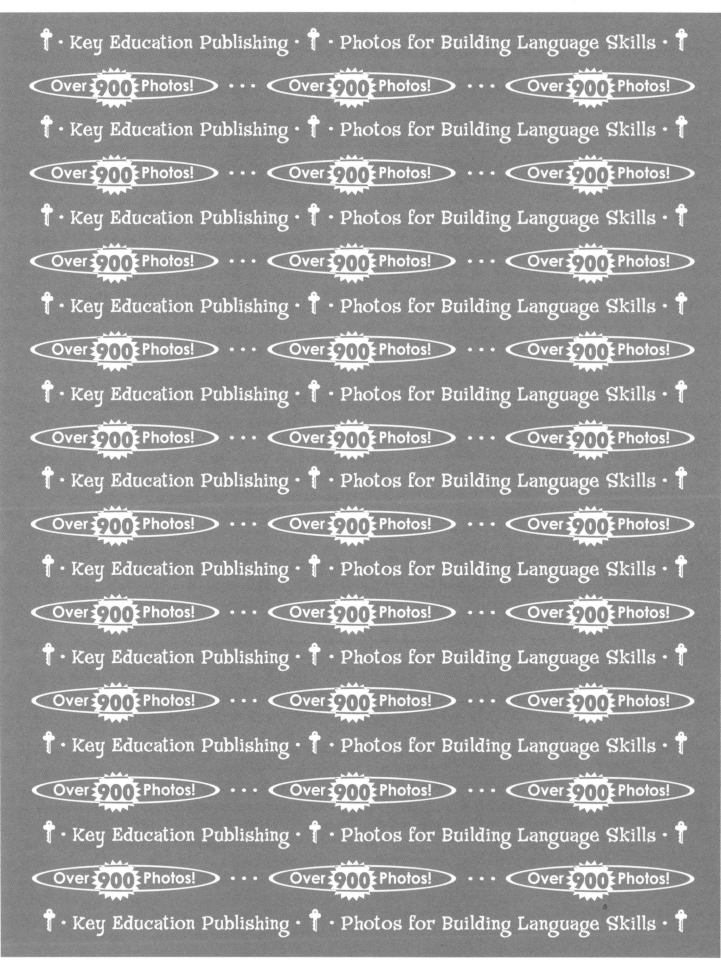

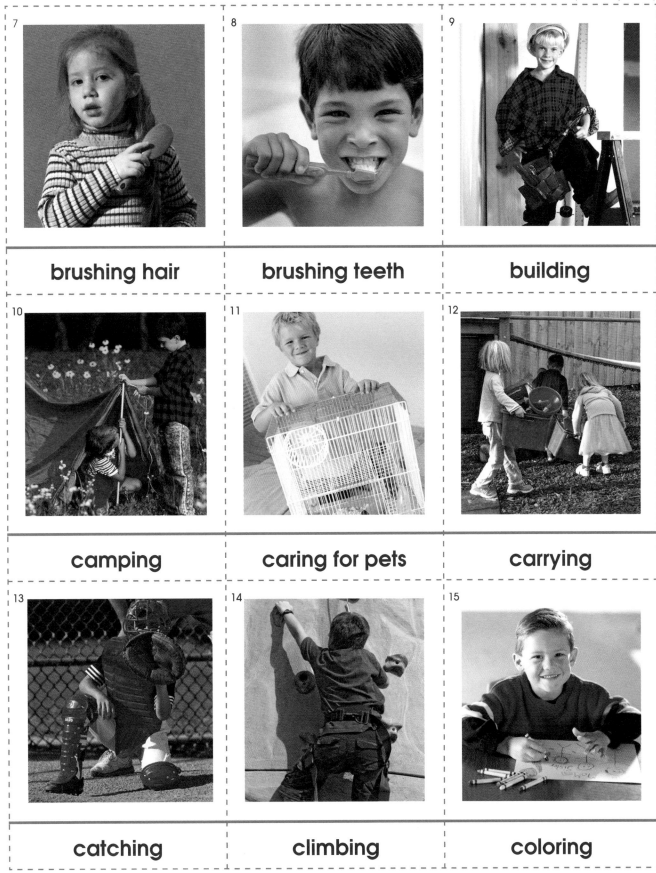

brushing hair	**brushing teeth**	**building**
camping	**caring for pets**	**carrying**
catching	**climbing**	**coloring**

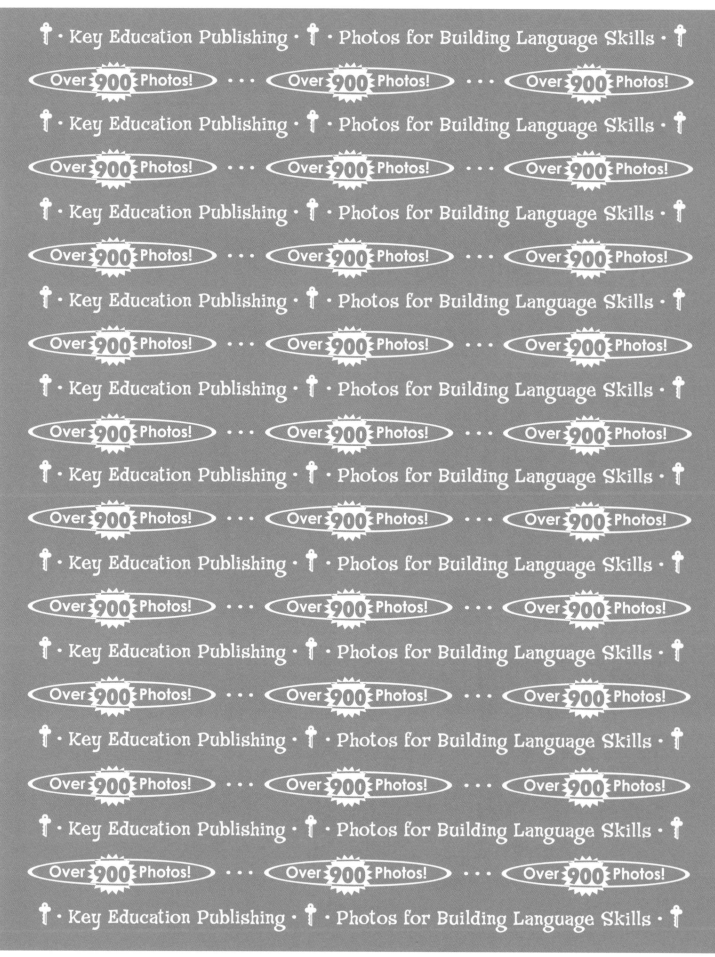

16	17	18
cooking	**crawling**	**crying**
19	20	21
cutting	**dancing**	**digging**
22	23	24
drawing	**drinking**	**driving**

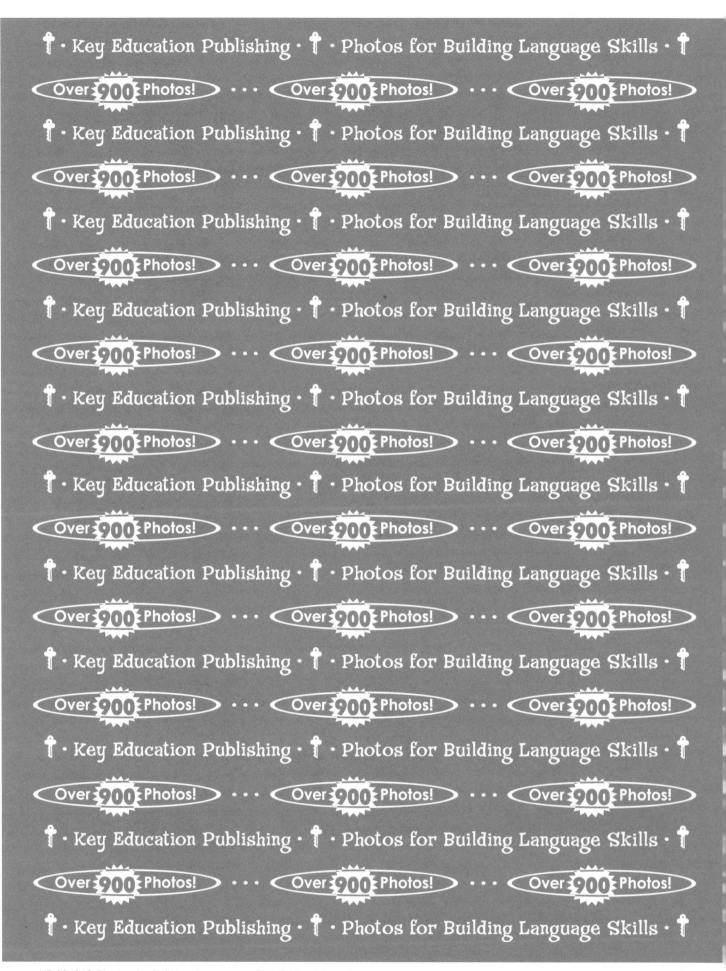

25	26	27
eating	feeding	fishing
28	29	30
floating	gardening	giving
31	32	33
grilling	hanging	hiding

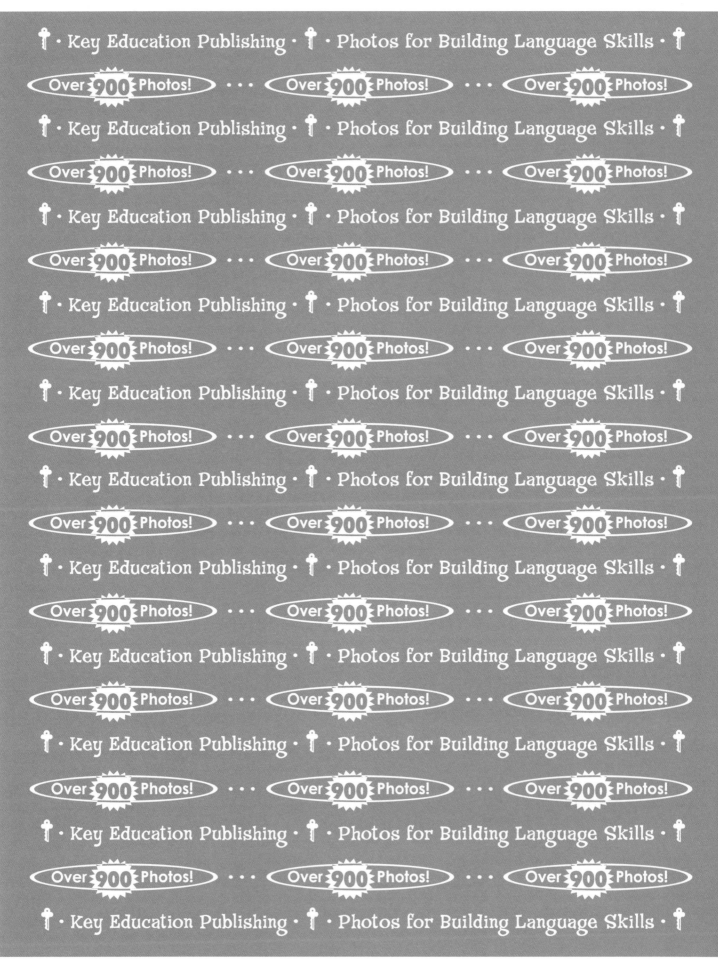

34	35	36
hitting	**holding hands**	**hopping**

37	38	39
hugging	**jumping**	**kicking**

40	41	42
kissing	**laughing**	**licking**

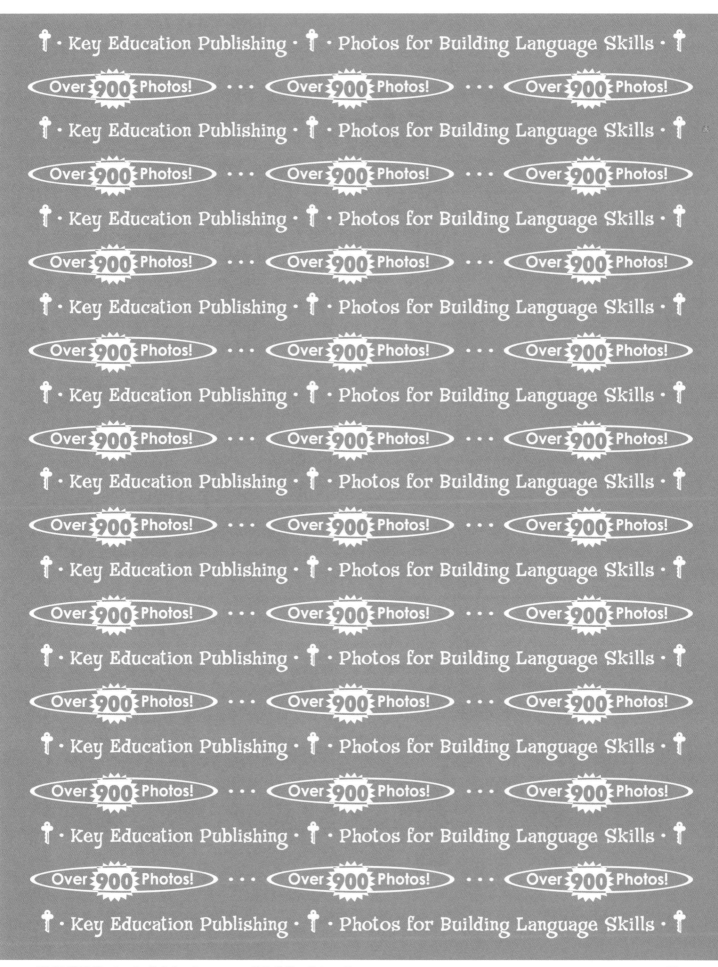

43	44	45
looking	**marching**	**molding clay**
46	47	48
paddling	**painting**	**peeking**
49	50	51
petting	**picking**	**playing (boy)**

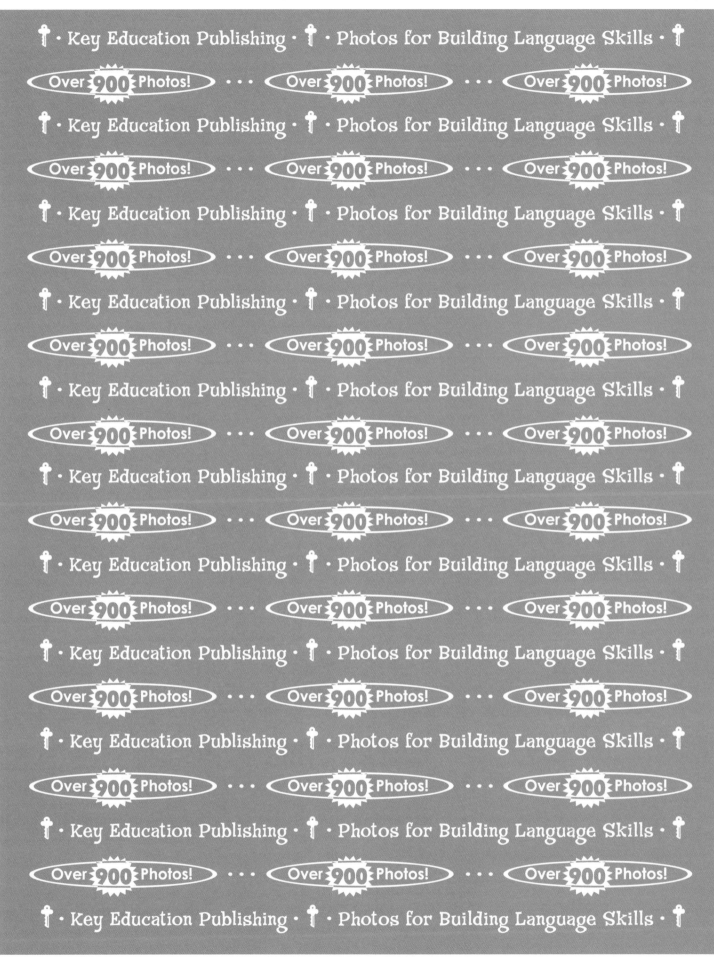

playing (girl)

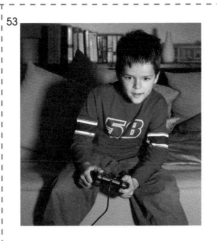

playing video games

pointing

pouring

praying

pretending

pulling

putting away

raising hand

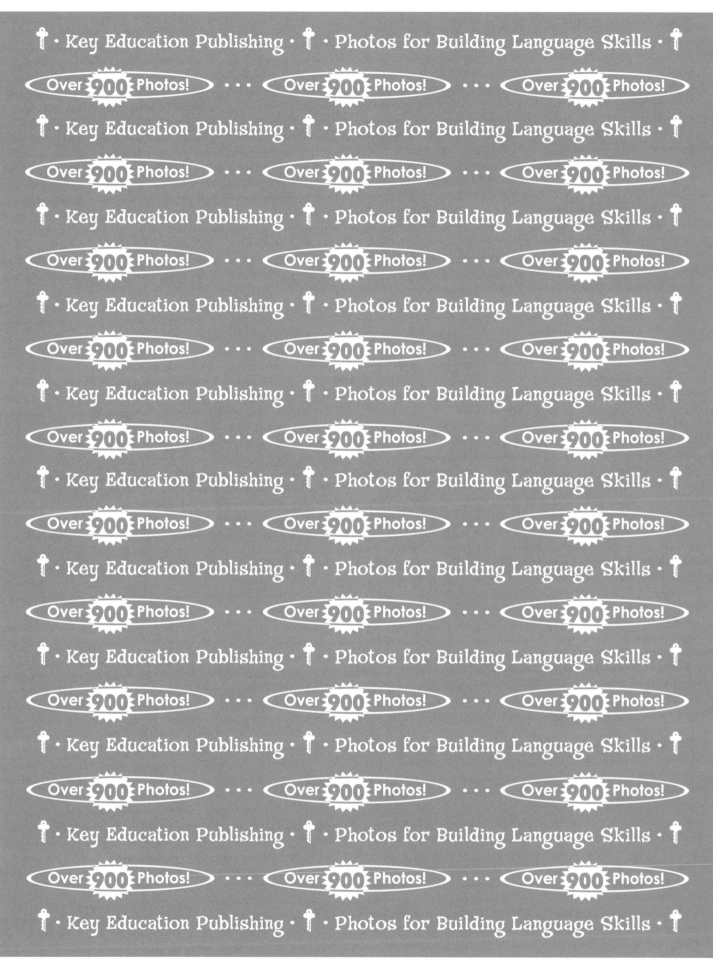

raking	reading	riding
rolling	running	scolding
sharing	shopping	singing

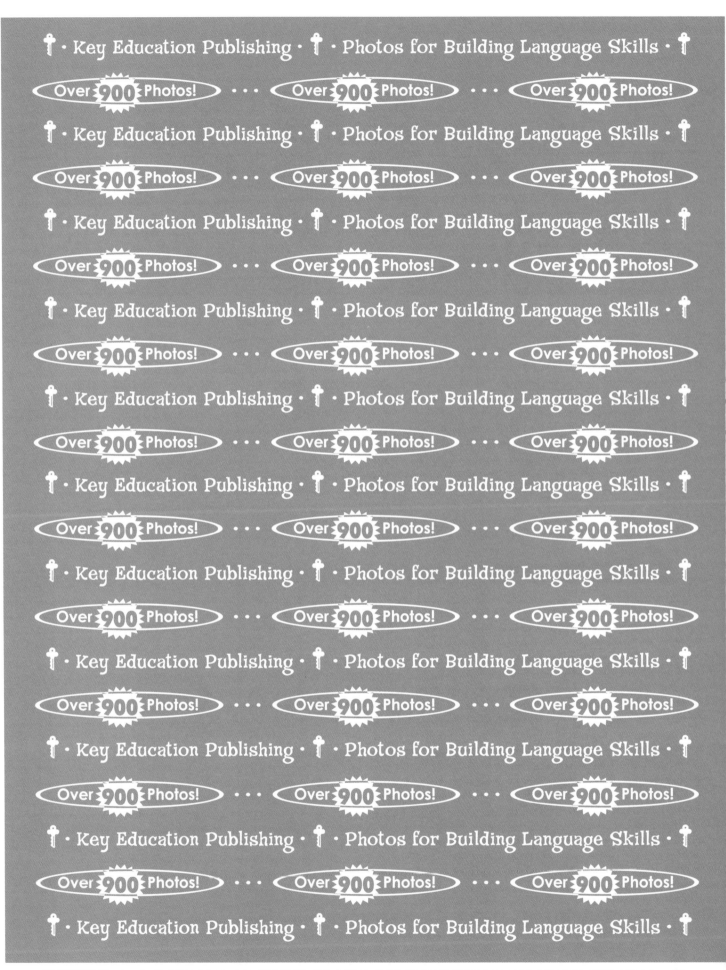

70	71	72
sitting	skating	skiing
73	74	75
skipping	sleeping	sliding
76	77	78
smelling	smiling	sneezing

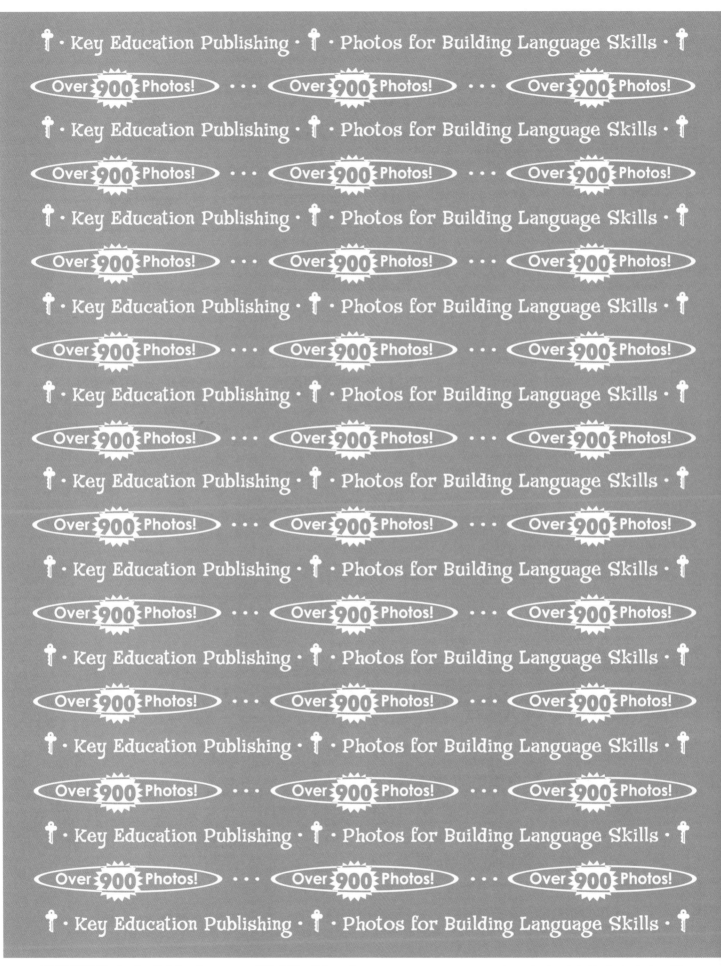

79 splashing

80 stacking

81 sucking thumb

82 swimming

83 swinging

84 talking

85 thinking

86 throwing

87 tickling

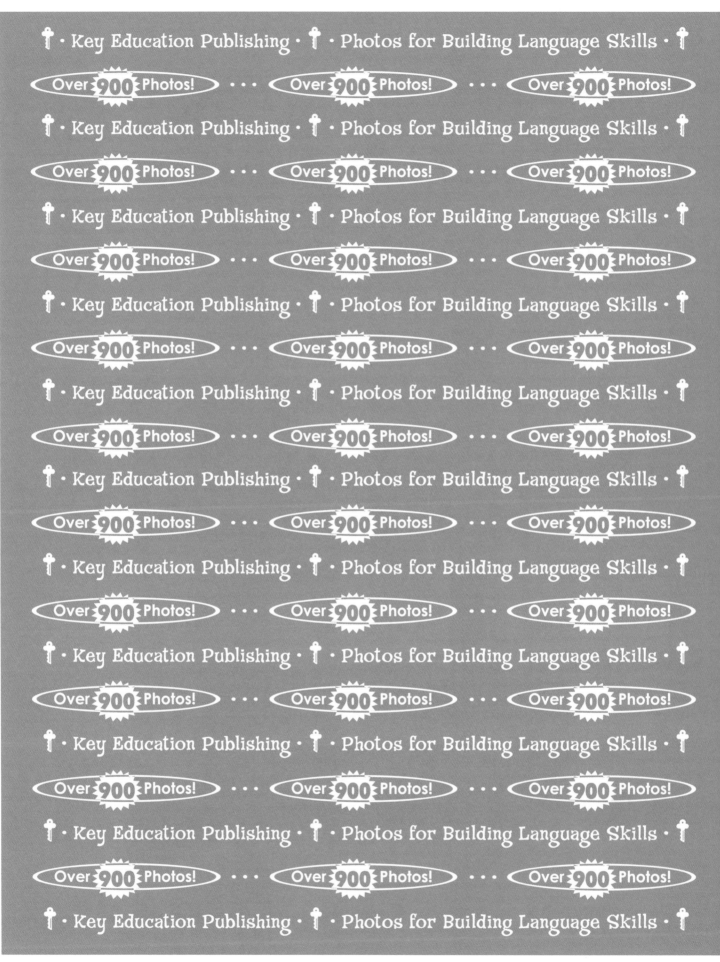

88	89	90
tying shoes	**typing**	**walking**
91	92	93
washing car	**washing hands**	**watching TV**
94	95	96
waving	**writing**	**zipping**

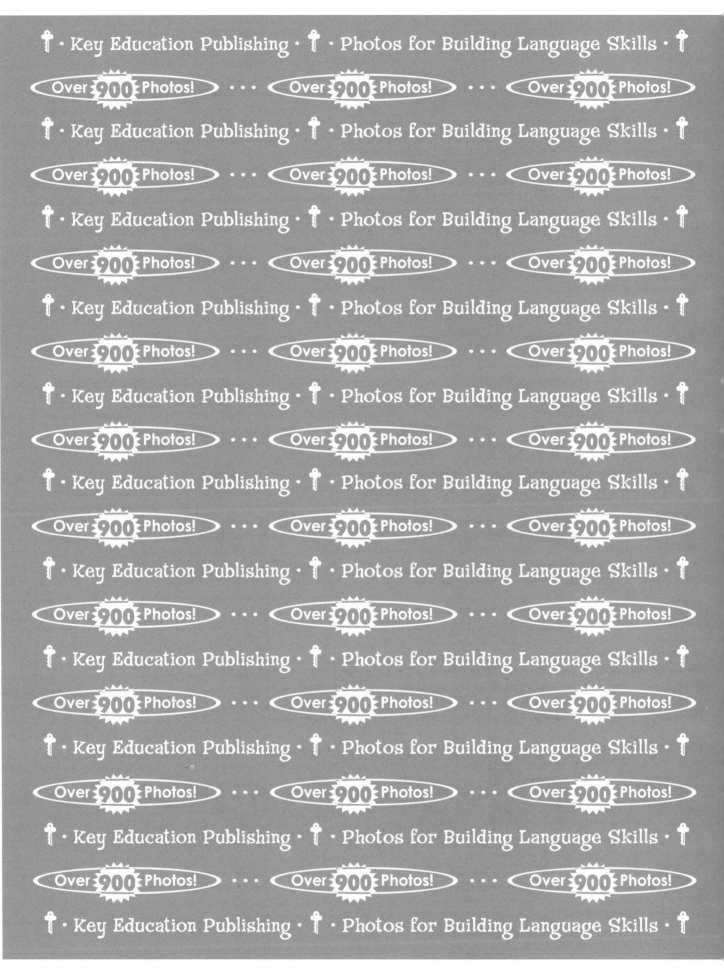

Chapter 2: Animals

The animal cards (pages 33 through 45) and the following sorting and sequencing activities can encourage expressive language, increase vocabulary, and build observational skills.

1. Sort the animal cards by where the animals might live, such as:
   - farm animals
   - wild animals
   - animals that live in a cold climate
   - animals that live in a warm climate
   - jungle animals
   - forest animals
   - animals that live in trees
   - animals that live in caves
   - backyard animals
   - animals that live in or near water
   - animals that live in the desert

2. Sequence the animals by size, such as largest to smallest or tallest to shortest.

3. Sort the animals by their colors, such as brown, black, white, multicolored, spotted, stripped, or patterns.

4. Sort the animals by textures, such as animals with feathers, animals with fur, animals with skin, animals with scales, or animals with a shell.

5. Sort the animals by what you think each animal would feel like, such as: soft, hard, sharp, smooth, rough, scratchy, prickly, furry, or woolly.

6. Sort the animals by the number of legs, such as 4 legs, 2 legs, 8 legs, or no legs.

1 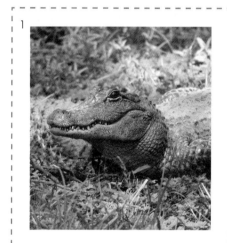	2 	3 
alligator	**ant**	**bear**
4 	5 	6 
bee	**bird**	**butterfly**

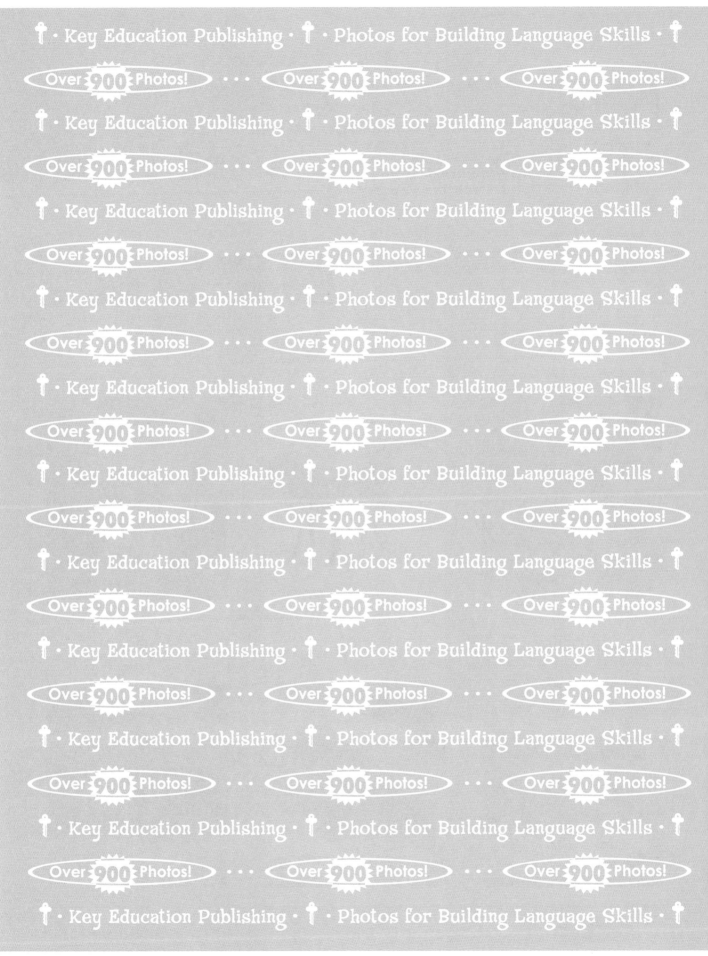

cat	chick	chicken
chimpanzee	cow	deer
dog	dolphin	donkey

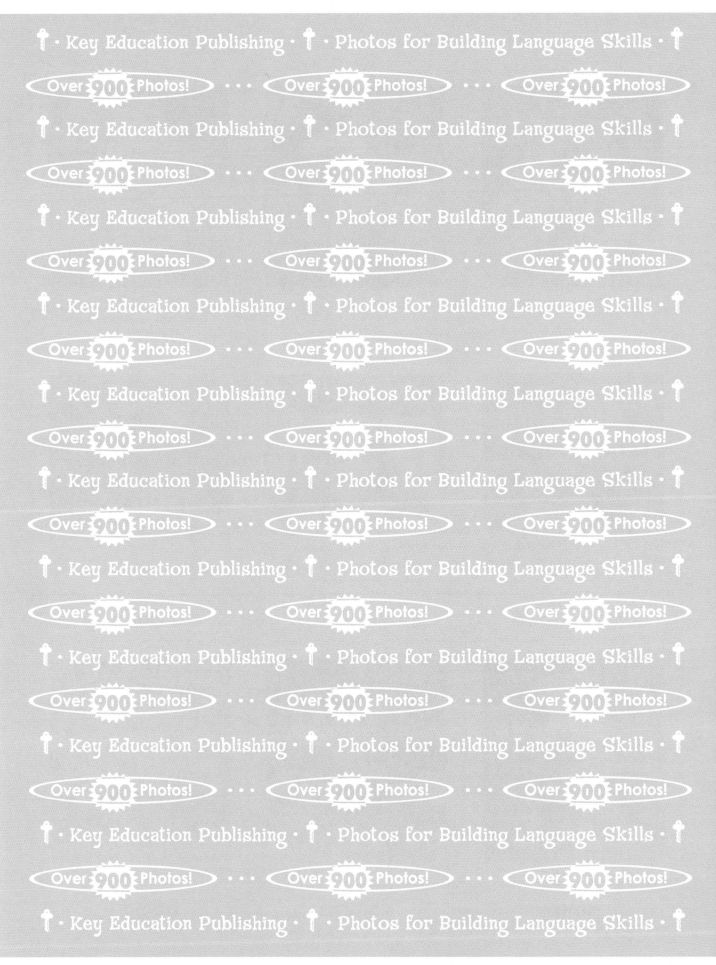

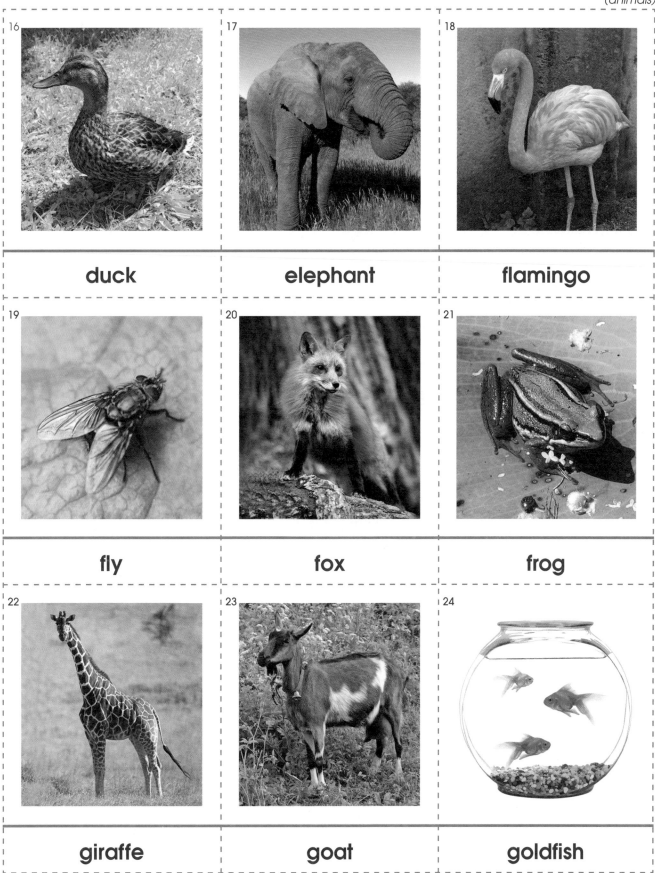

duck	elephant	flamingo
fly	fox	frog
giraffe	goat	goldfish

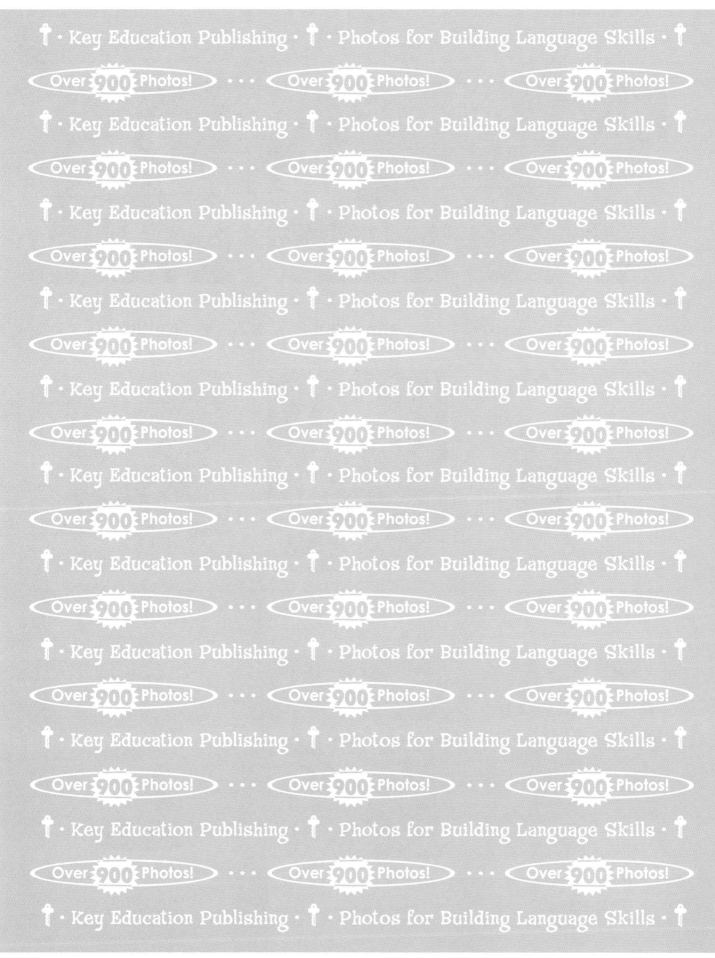

25 gorilla	26 grasshopper	27 guinea pig
28 hippopotamus	29 horse	30 kangaroo
31 kitten	32 koala	33 ladybug

34	35	36
lion	macaw	moose
37	38	39
mouse	orangutan	ostrich
40	41	42
owl	panda	penguin

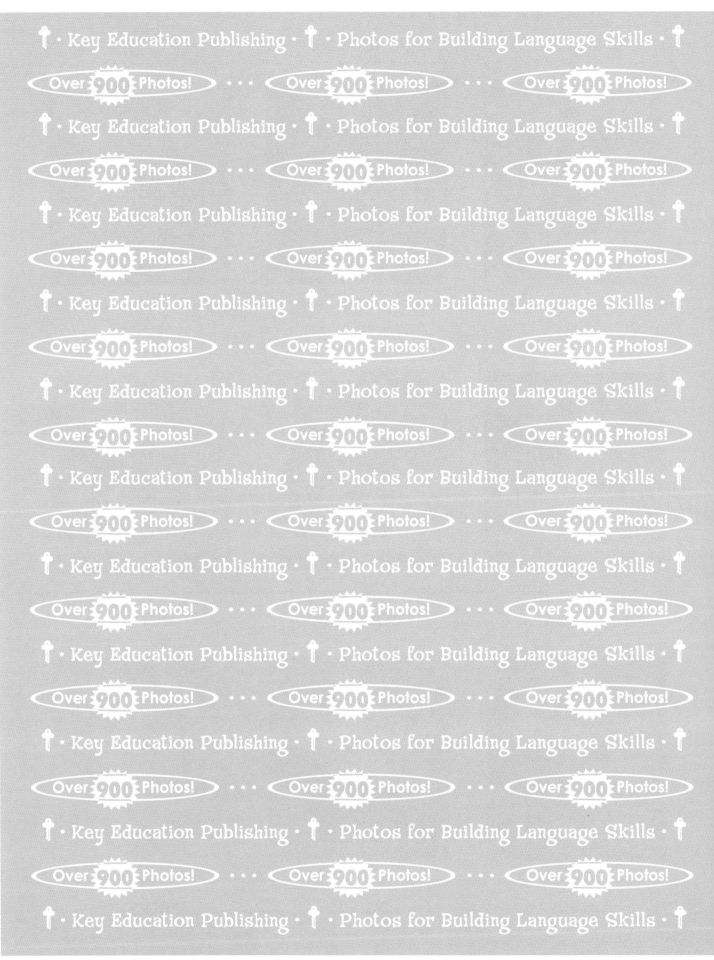

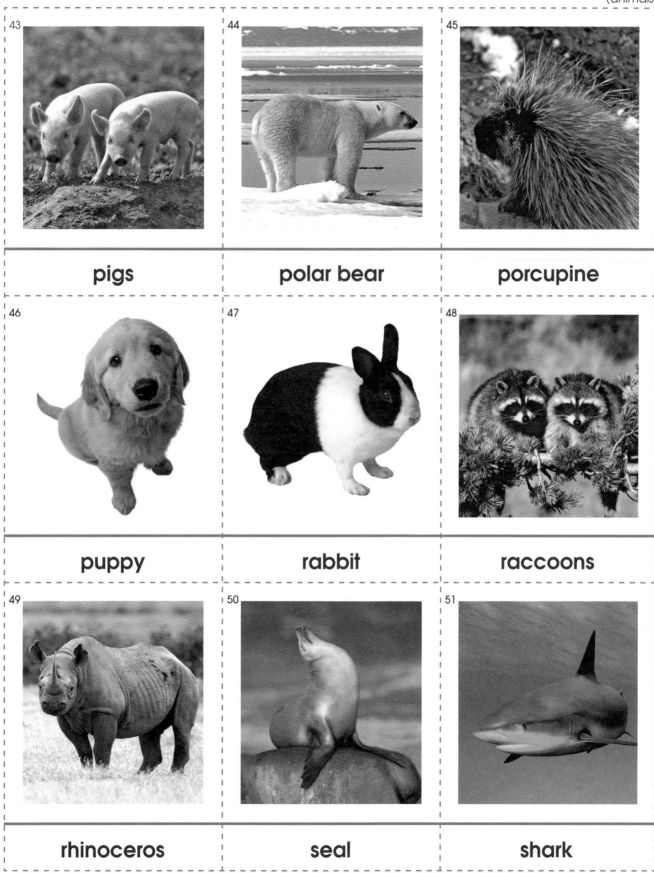

43 pigs

44 polar bear

45 porcupine

46 puppy

47 rabbit

48 raccoons

49 rhinoceros

50 seal

51 shark

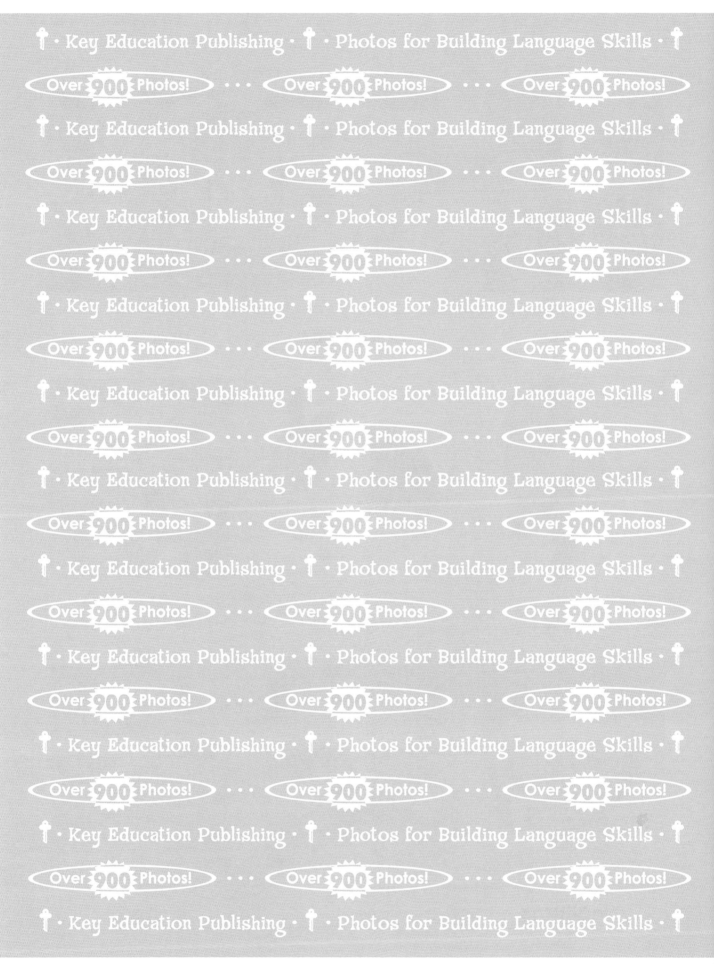

52 sheep	53 skunk	54 snake
55 spider	56 swan	57 tiger
58 walrus	59 whale	60 zebra

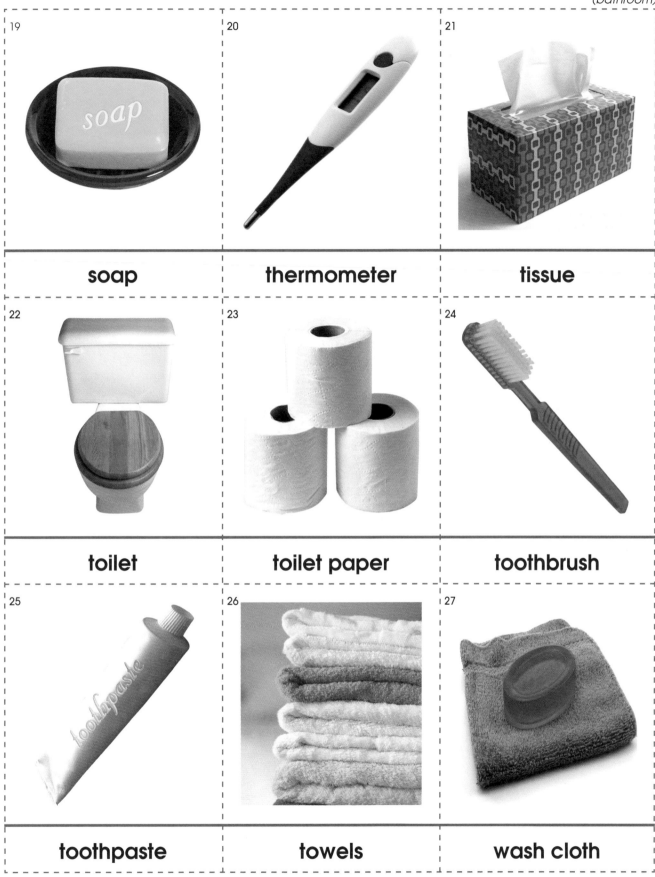

19	20	21
soap	**thermometer**	**tissue**
22	23	24
toilet	**toilet paper**	**toothbrush**
25	26	27
toothpaste	**towels**	**wash cloth**

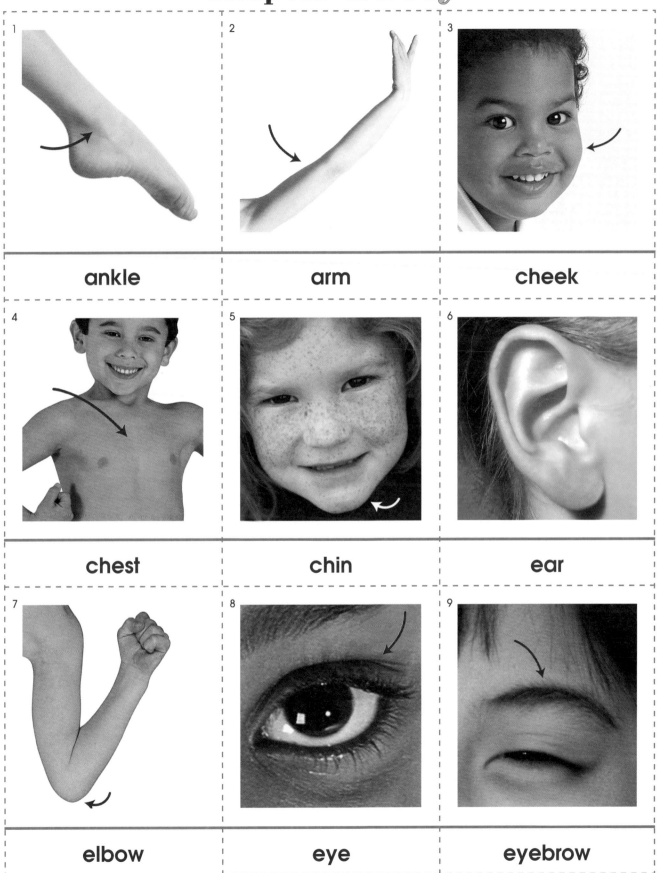

1 ankle	2 arm	3 cheek
4 chest	5 chin	6 ear
7 elbow	8 eye	9 eyebrow

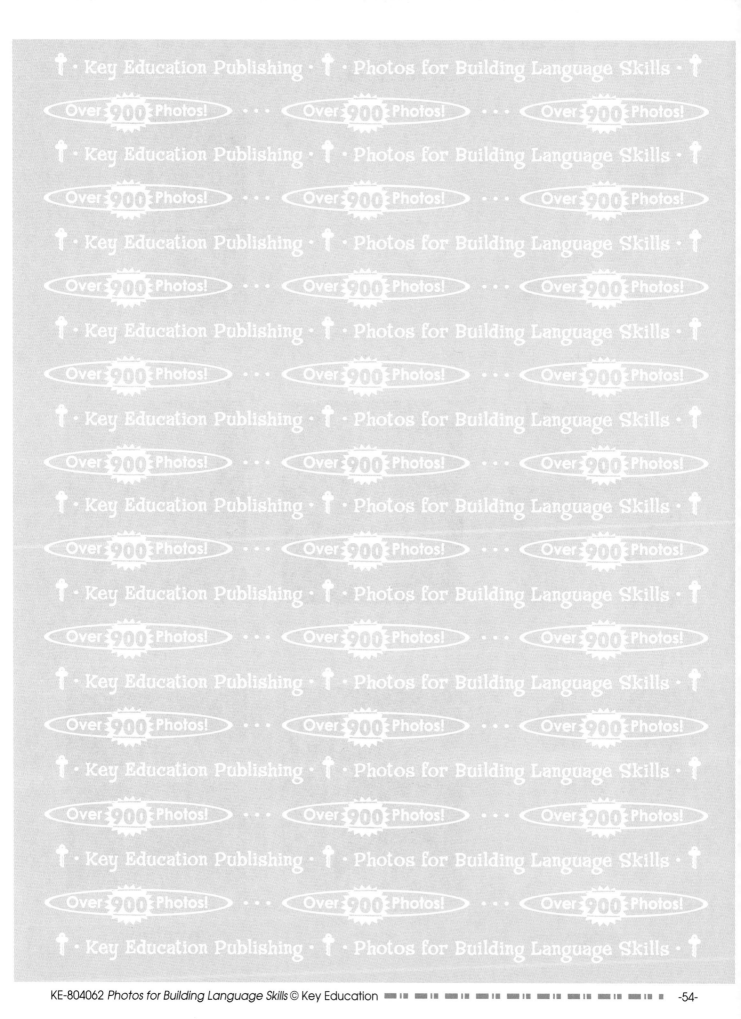

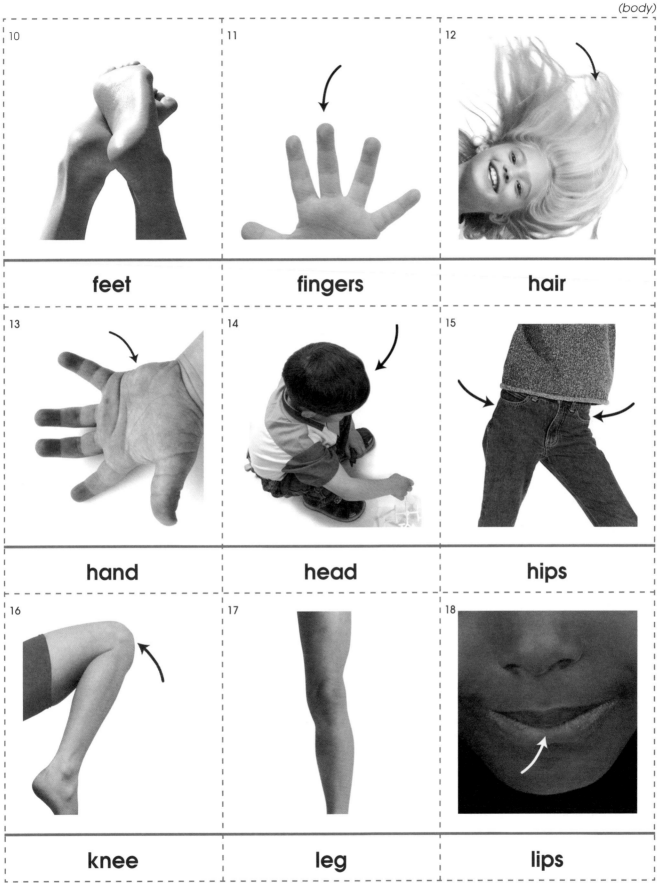

10	11	12
feet	fingers	hair
13	14	15
hand	head	hips
16	17	18
knee	leg	lips

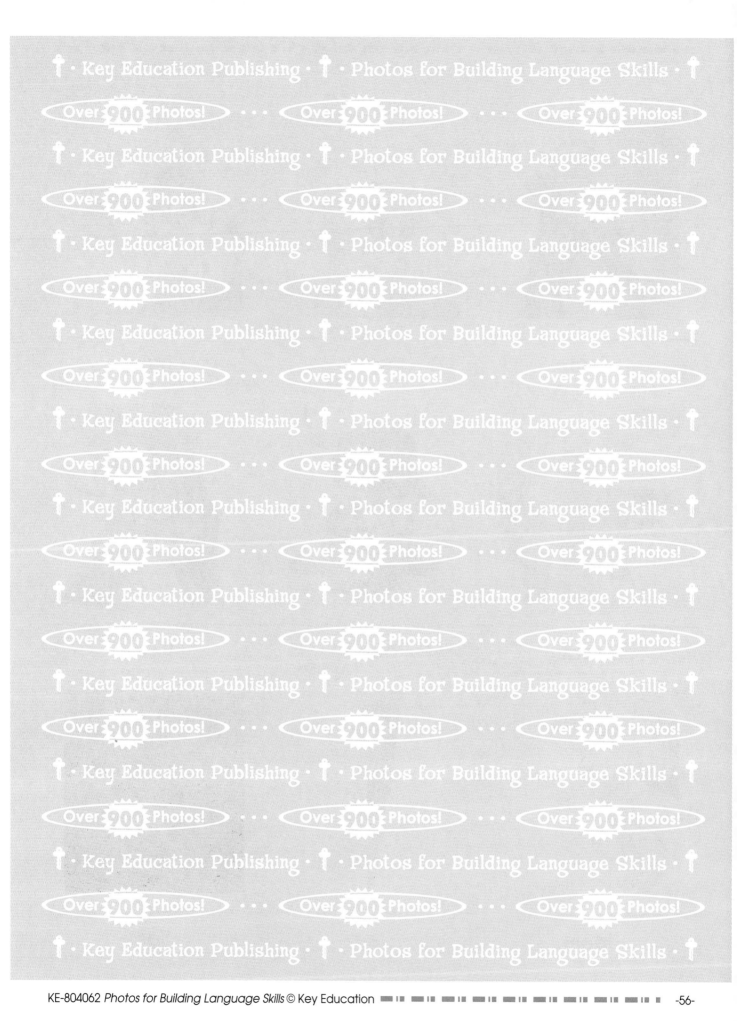

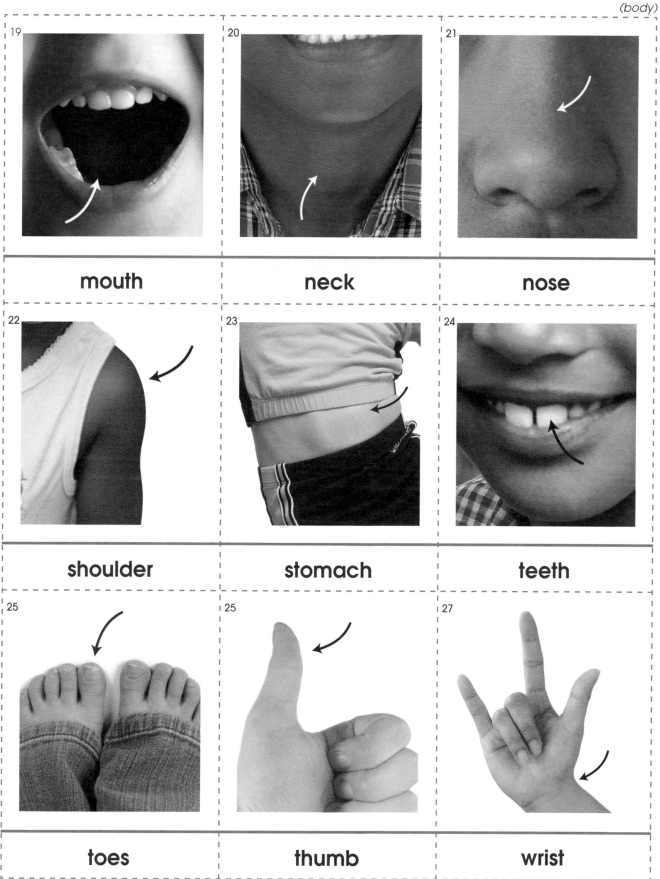

mouth	neck	nose
shoulder	stomach	teeth
toes	thumb	wrist

Chapter 5: Clothing

1	2	3
belt	blouse	boots
4	5	6
bow tie	cap	dress
7	8	9
dress shoes (boys)	dress shoes (girls)	flip flops

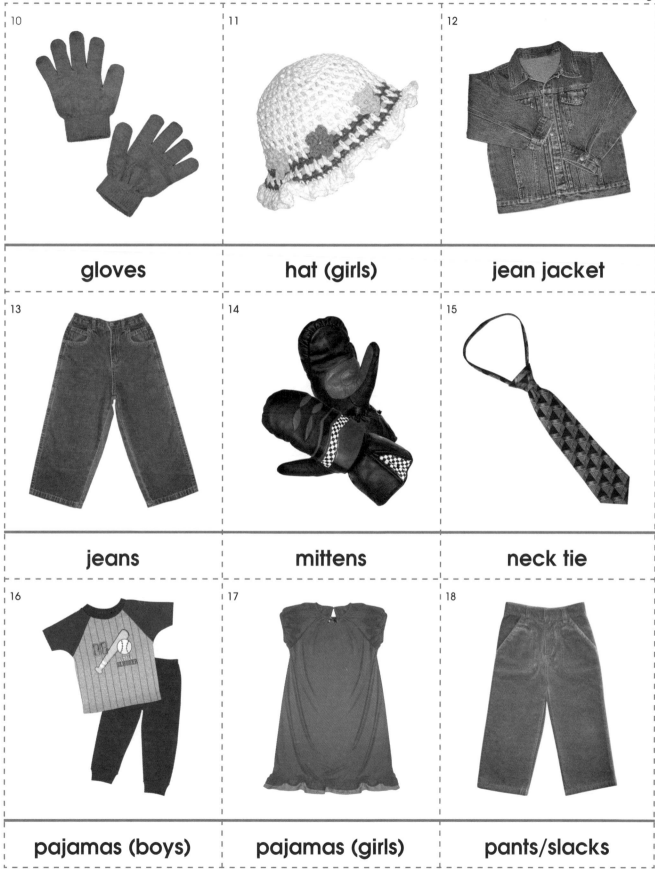

10

gloves

11

hat (girls)

12

jean jacket

13

jeans

14

mittens

15

neck tie

16

pajamas (boys)

17

pajamas (girls)

18

pants/slacks

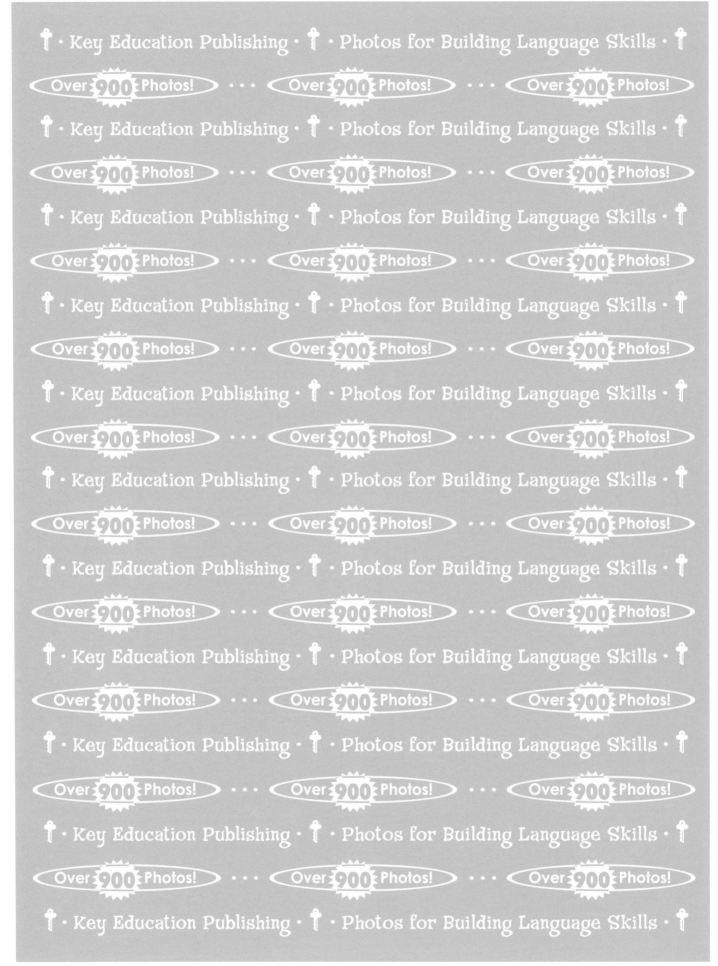

19 **purse**	20 **raincoat**	21 **robe**
22 **sandals**	23 **scarf**	24 **shirt (boys)**
25 **shorts**	26 **skirt**	27 **slippers**

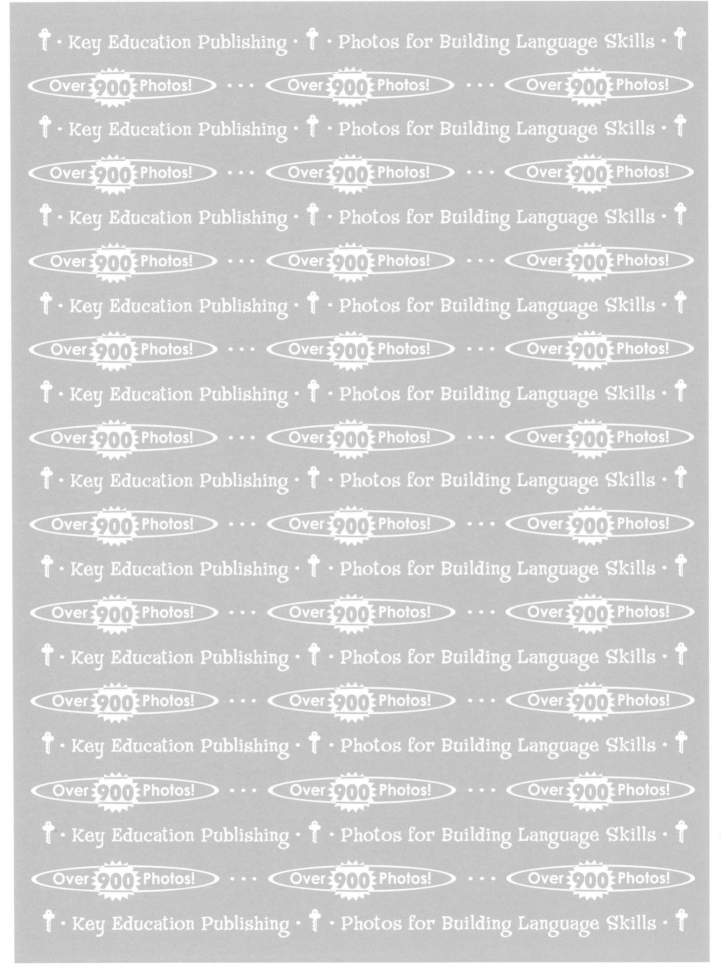

28	29	30
socks	**sunglasses**	**sweat pants**
31	32	33
sweat shirt	**sweater**	**swimsuit (boys)**
34	35	36
swimsuit (girls)	**t-shirt**	**tennis shoes**

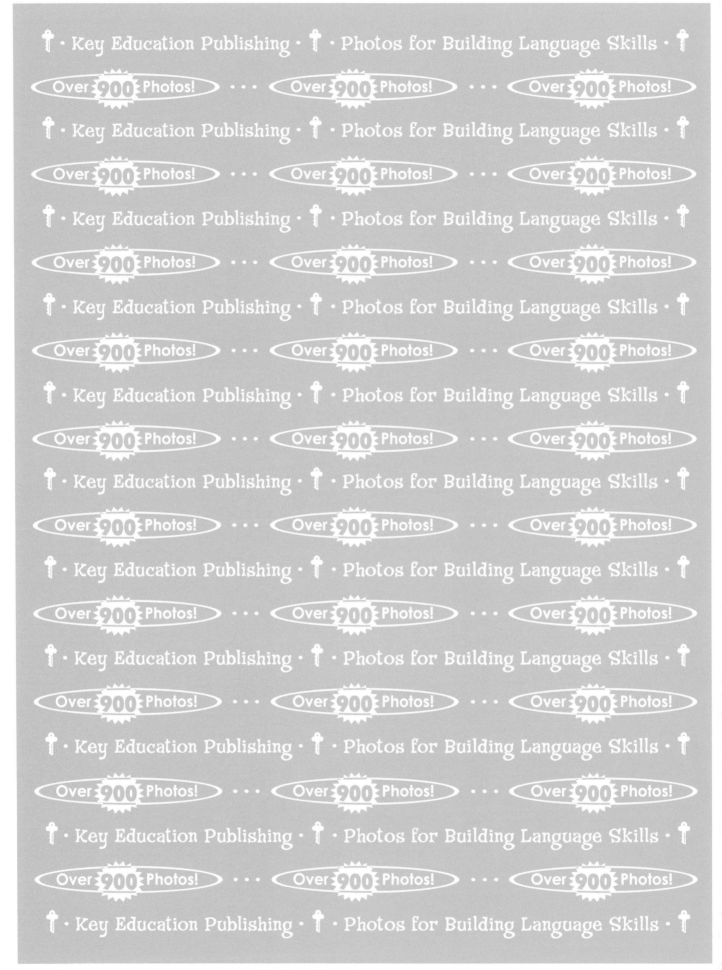

37	38	39
turtleneck	**umbrella**	**underwear/ boxer shorts**
40	41	42
underwear/panties	**vest**	**white shirt**
43	44	45
winter hat	**winter jacket (boys)**	**winter jacket (girls)**

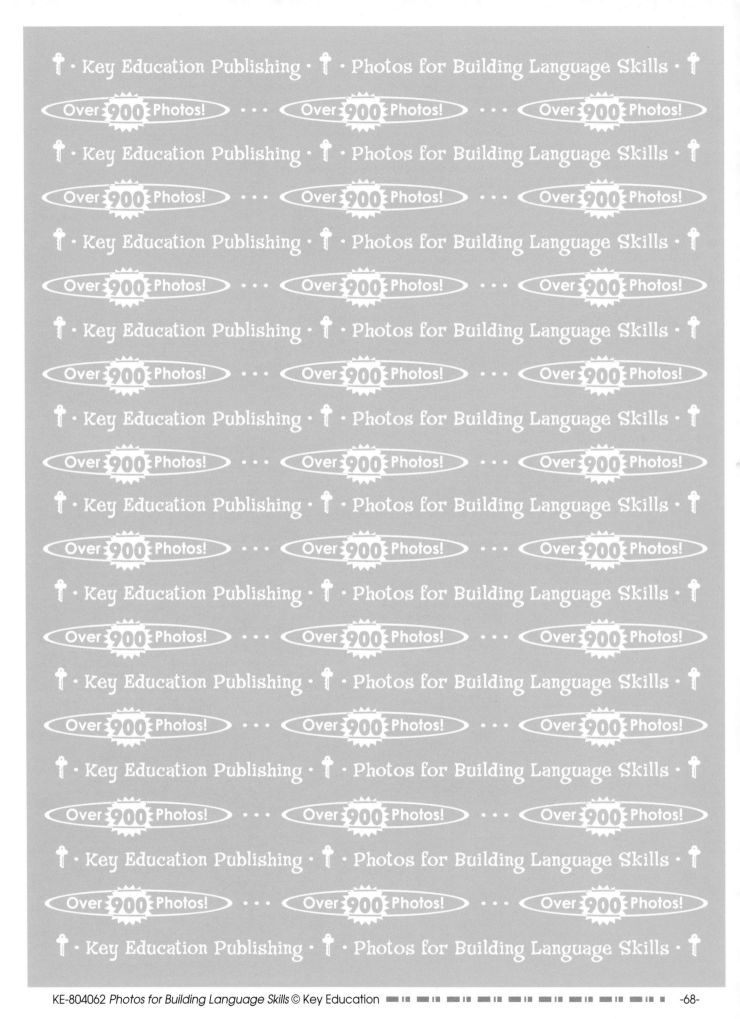

Chapter 6: Colors & Shapes

Matching Games

The color and shape matching lotto games are fun to play and can help children learn to identify colors and shapes. Make color lotto game boards by gluing colored construction paper onto card stock. Shape lotto game boards can be made by drawing shapes onto card stock. Use the color and shape cards provided on pages 69 through 73 as the playing cards. Other photographic cards throughout this book can also be used as playing cards. There are a variety of matching possibilities. Children can match color square to color square; colored objects to the color squares; shape to shape; or shaped objects to the shapes on the game boards. See the examples that are shown below.

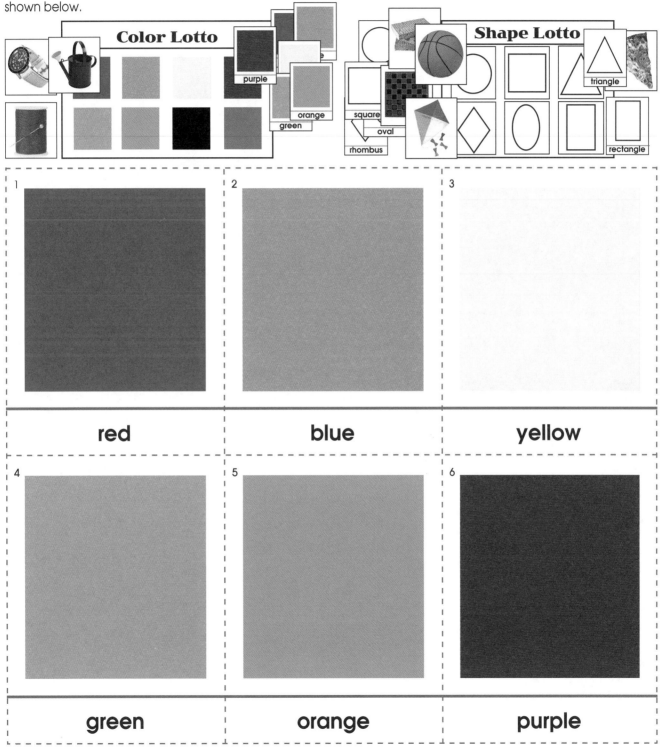

1 **red**	2 **blue**	3 **yellow**
4 **green**	5 **orange**	6 **purple**

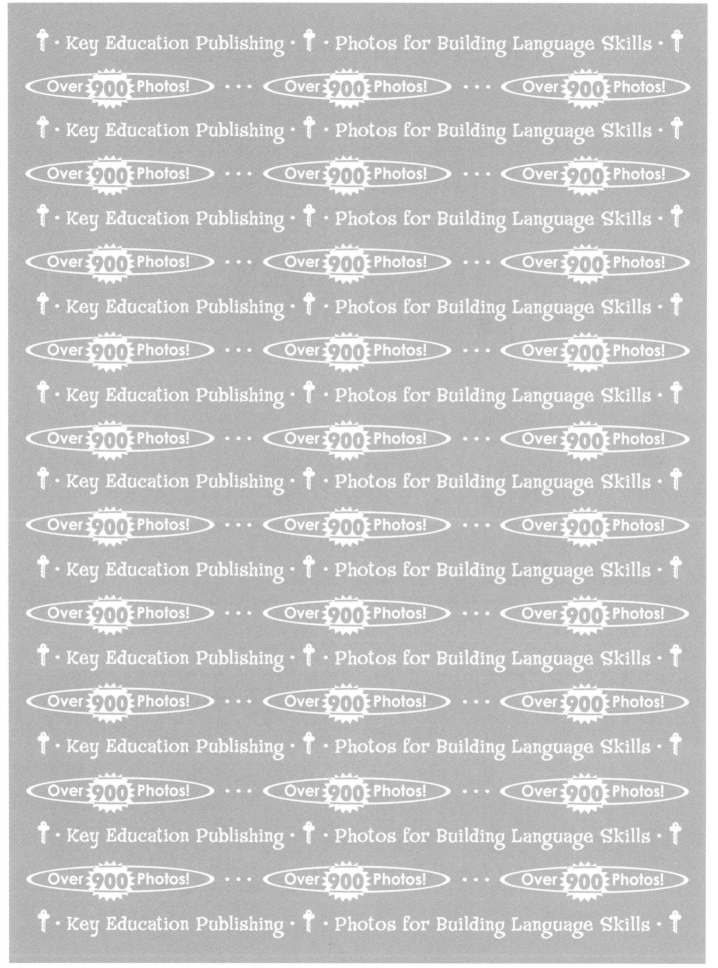

7	8	9
brown	**black**	**white**
10	11	12
pink	**gray**	**beige**
13	14	15
circle	**square**	**triangle**

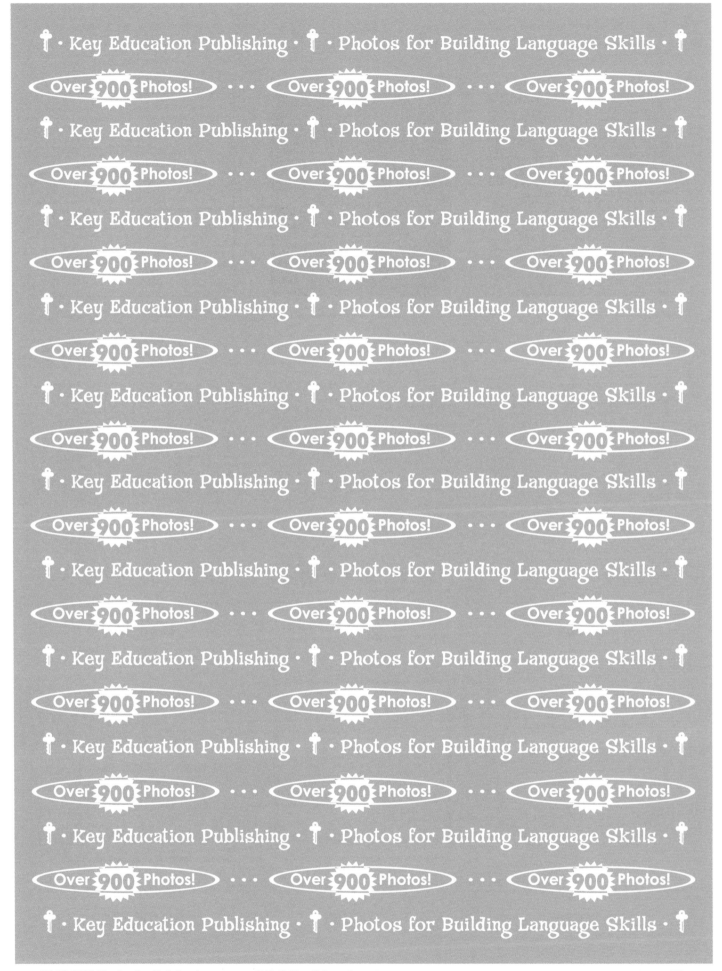

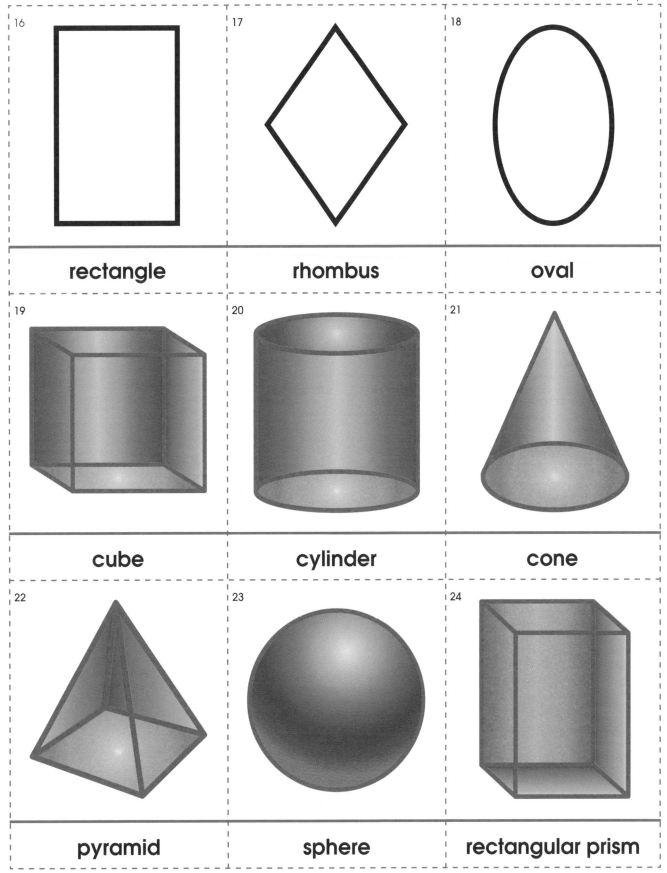

16	17	18
rectangle	rhombus	oval
19	20	21
cube	cylinder	cone
22	23	24
pyramid	sphere	rectangular prism

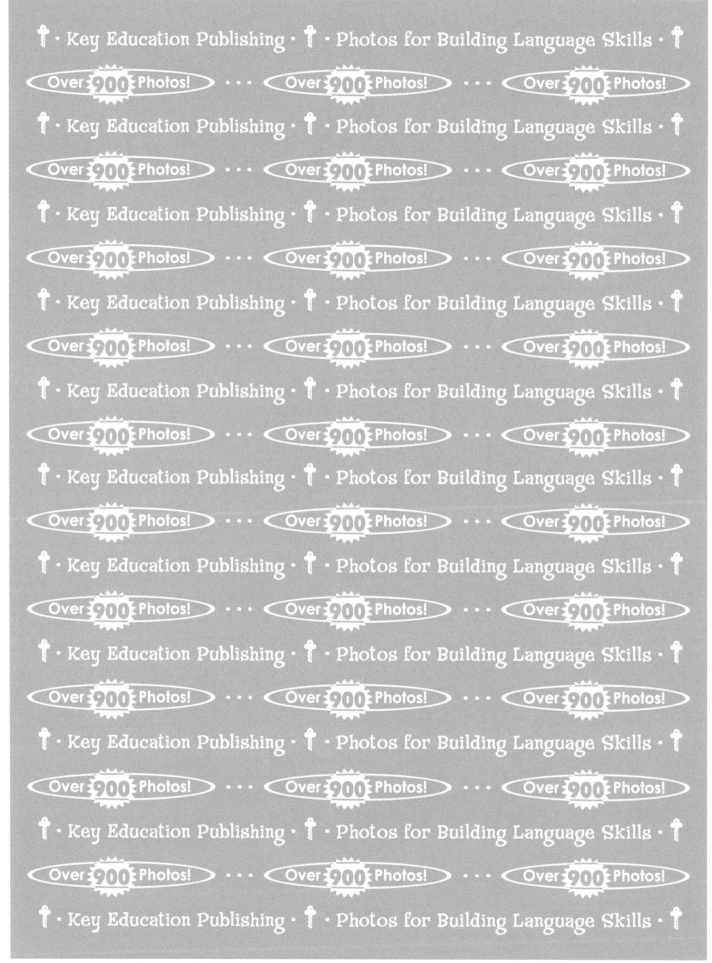

Chapter 7: Emotions

The cards found in Chapter 7 are photographs that depict a wide range of emotions. The following guided questions can help children increase their expressive language skills; recognize feelings in others; verbally describe how they are feeling; and enhance their ability to demonstrate empathy.

Show one card at a time. Ask the student various questions about the cards, such as;

- How to do think this child is feeling?
- Why do you think this child is feeling that way?
- Have you ever felt this way? When?
- What happened that made you feel like this?

Remember, there are no right or wrong answers. The children may see things in each of the pictures that you do not.

1

angry

2

bored

3

concerned

4

disgusted

5

excited

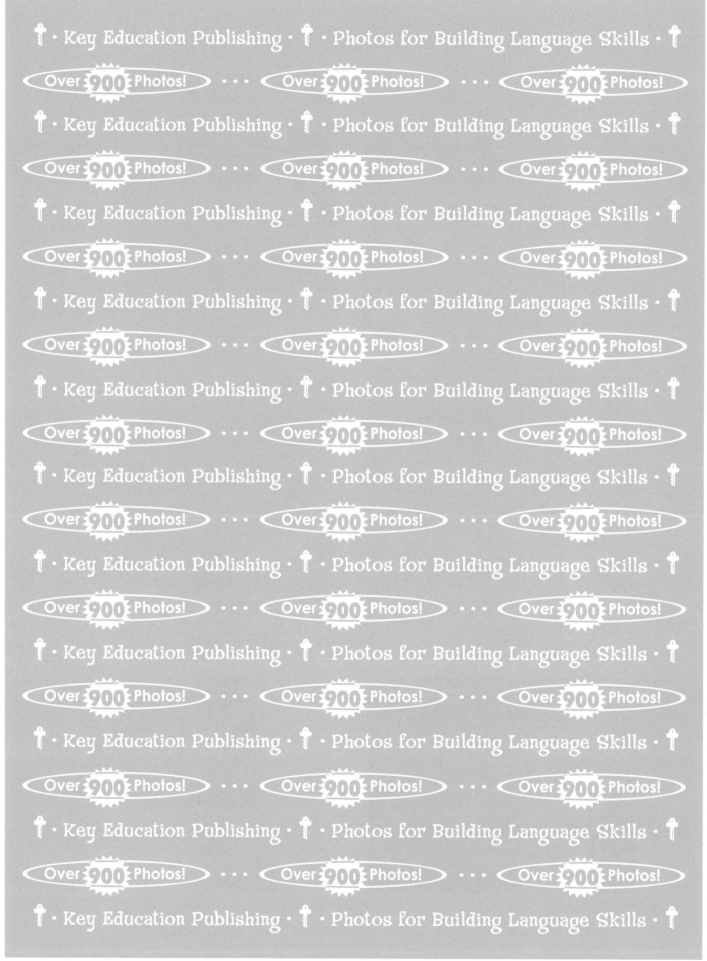

6
funny

7
happy

8
hurt

9
laughing

10
loving

11
mad

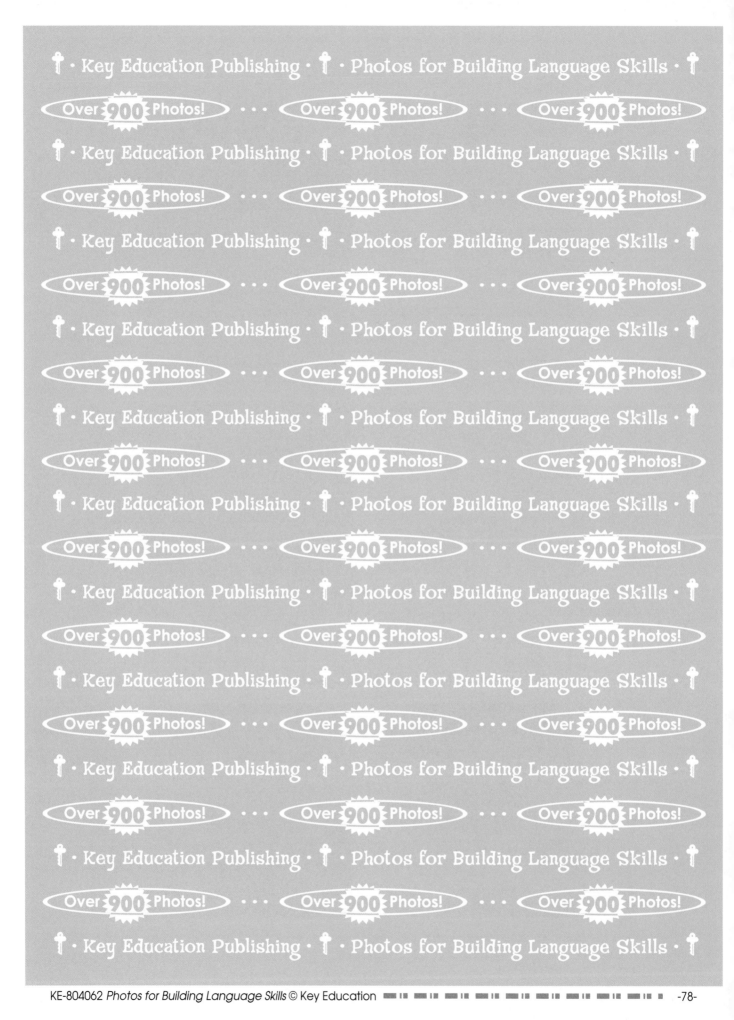

12 pouting

13 sad

14 scared

15 shocked

16 shy

17 sick

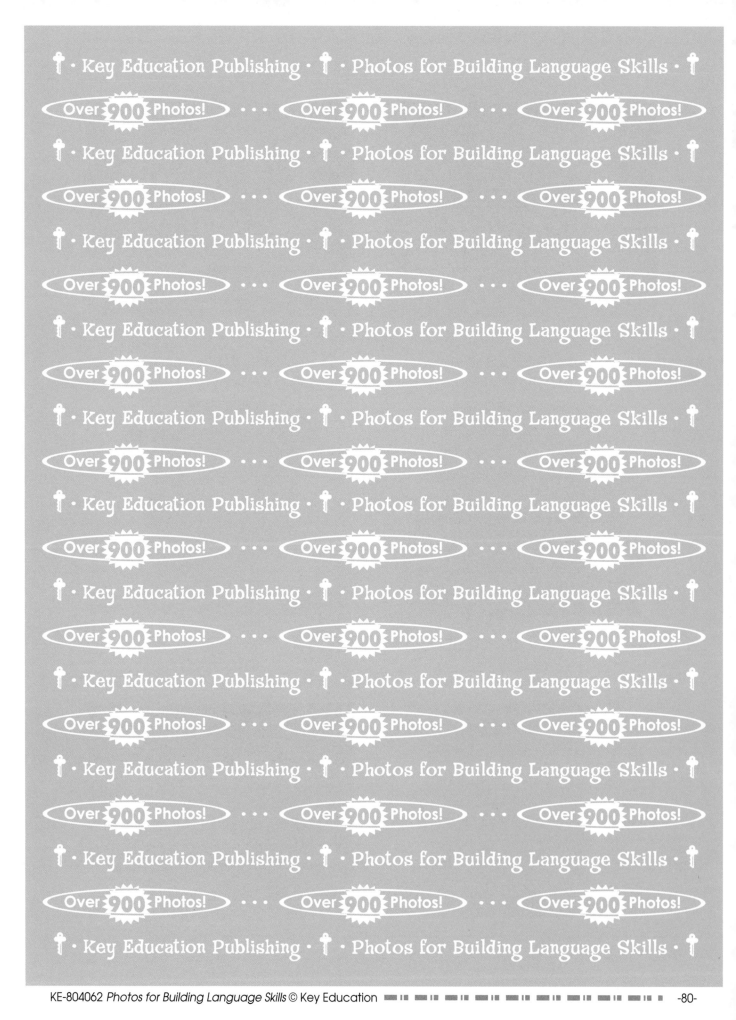

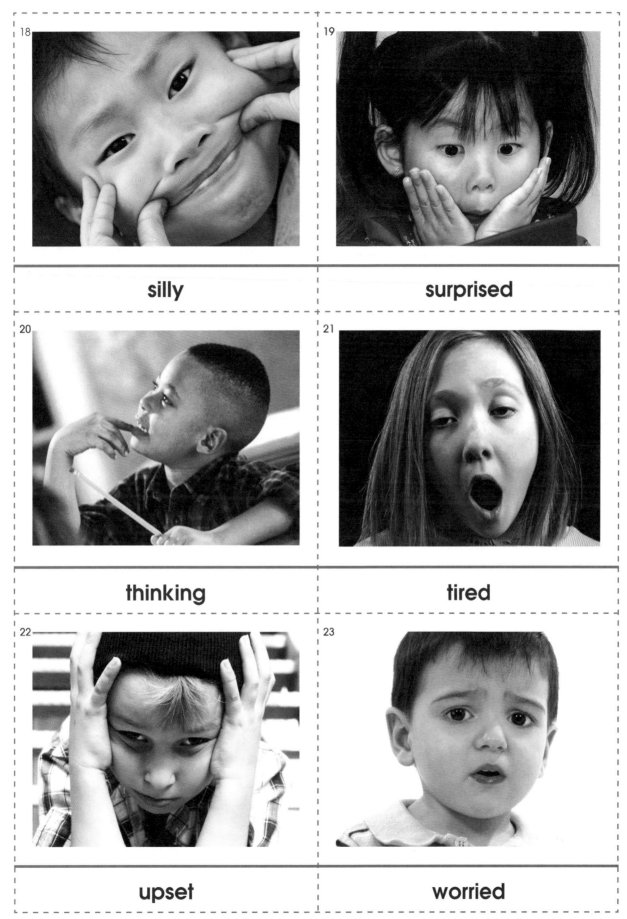

18

19

silly

surprised

20

21

thinking

tired

22

23

upset

worried

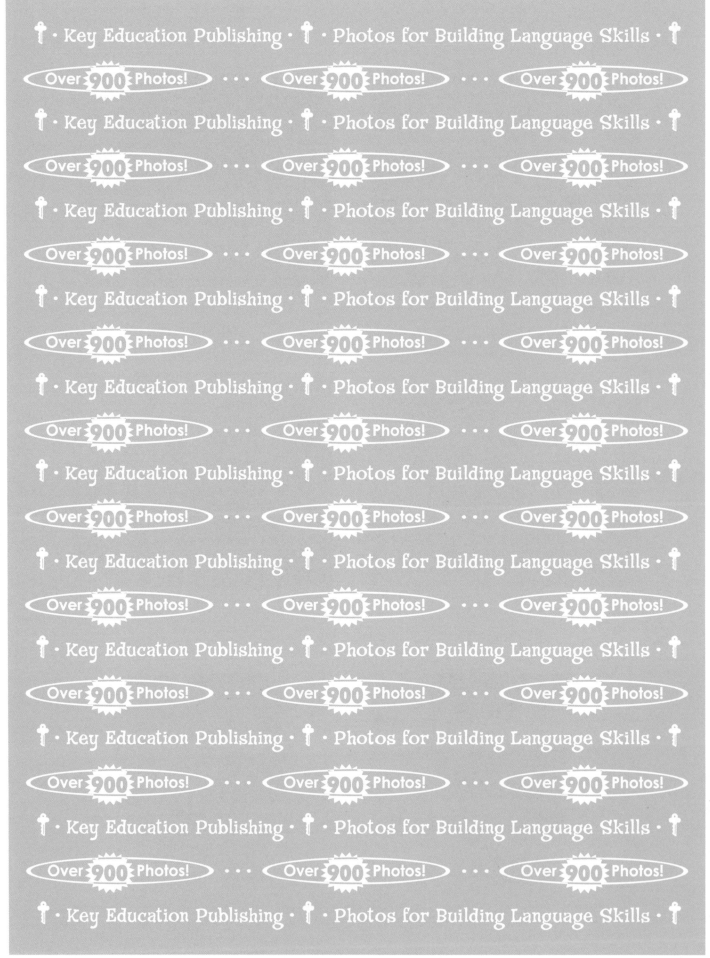

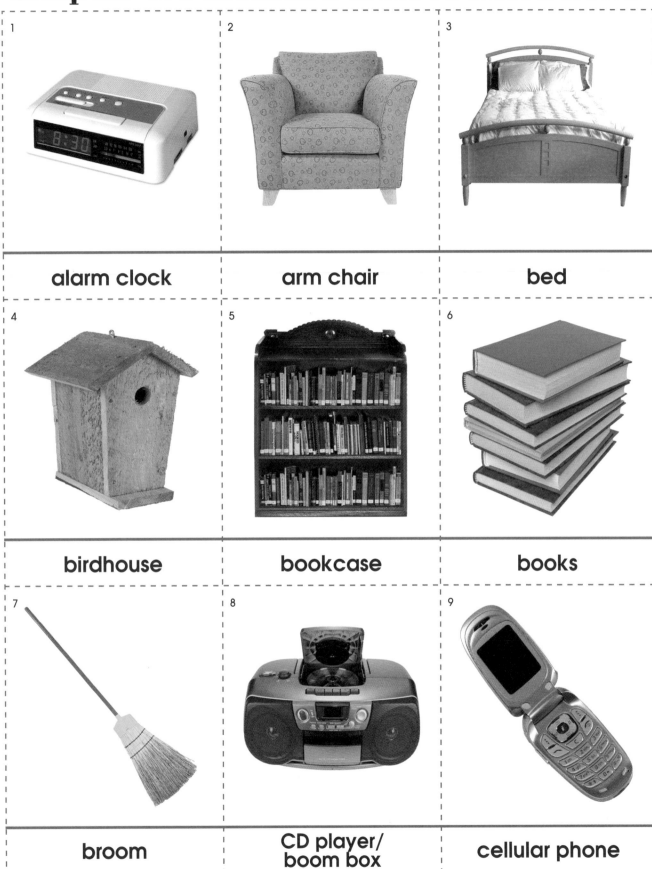

1	2	3
alarm clock	arm chair	bed
4	5	6
birdhouse	bookcase	books
7	8	9
broom	CD player/ boom box	cellular phone

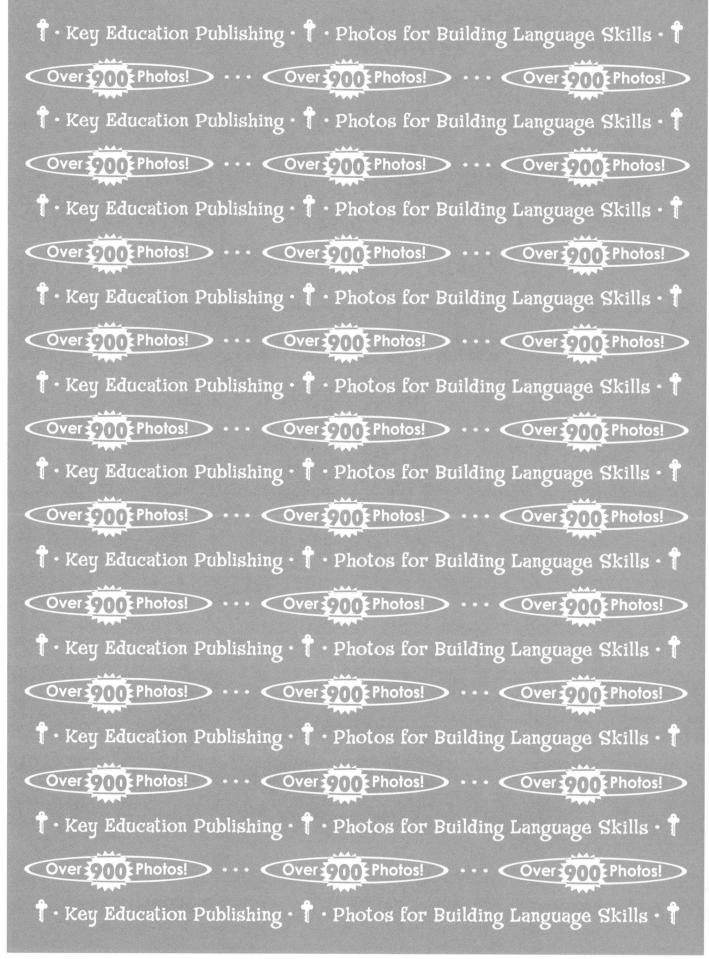

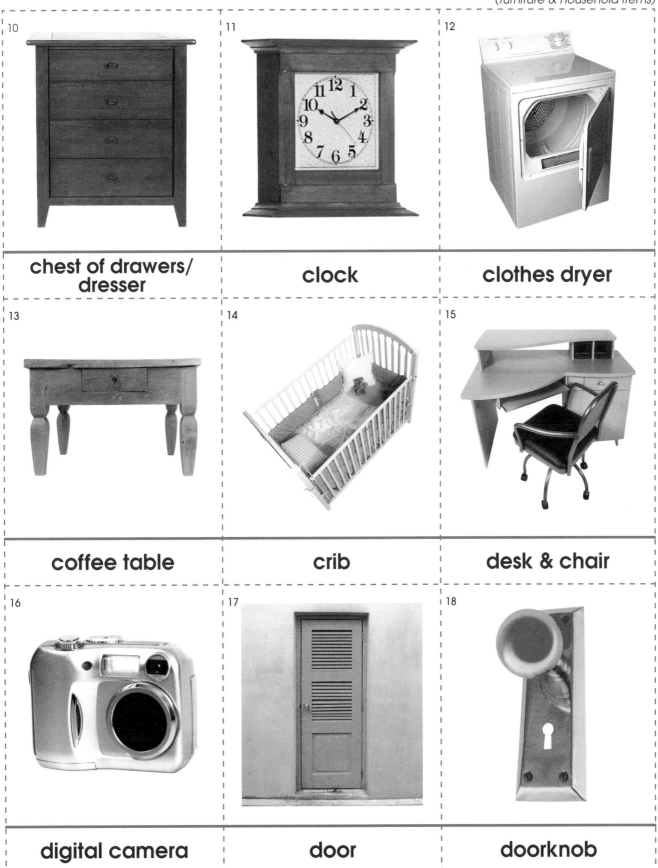

10	11	12
chest of drawers/ dresser	**clock**	**clothes dryer**
13	14	15
coffee table	**crib**	**desk & chair**
16	17	18
digital camera	**door**	**doorknob**

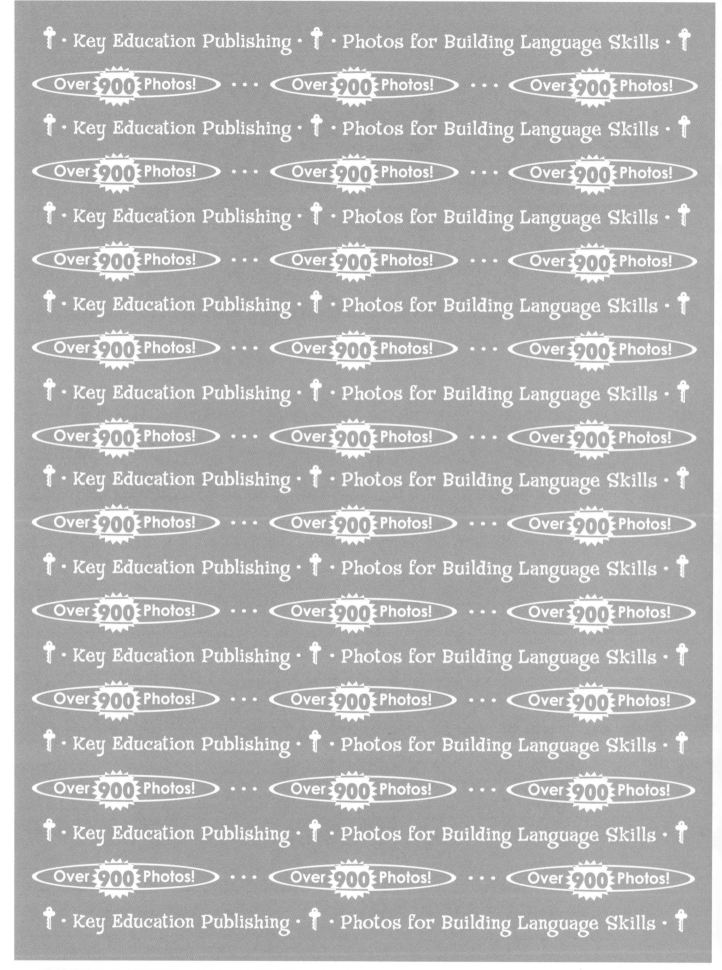

19	20	21
end table	**fan**	**flashlight**
22	23	24
flowers	**foot stool**	**gift/present**
25	26	27
hammer	**iron**	**ironing board**

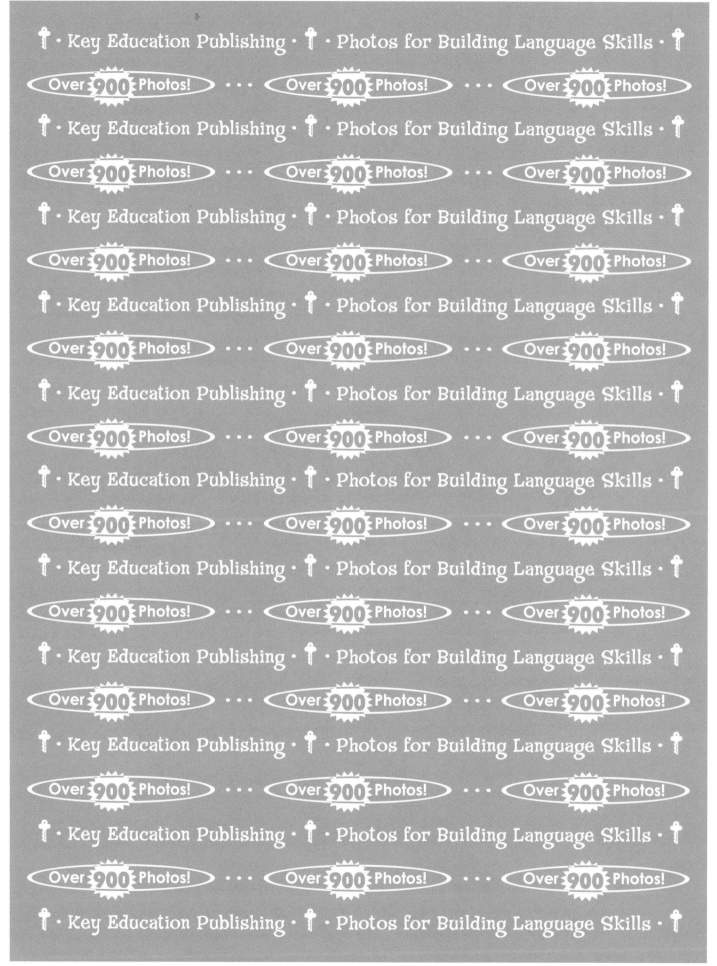

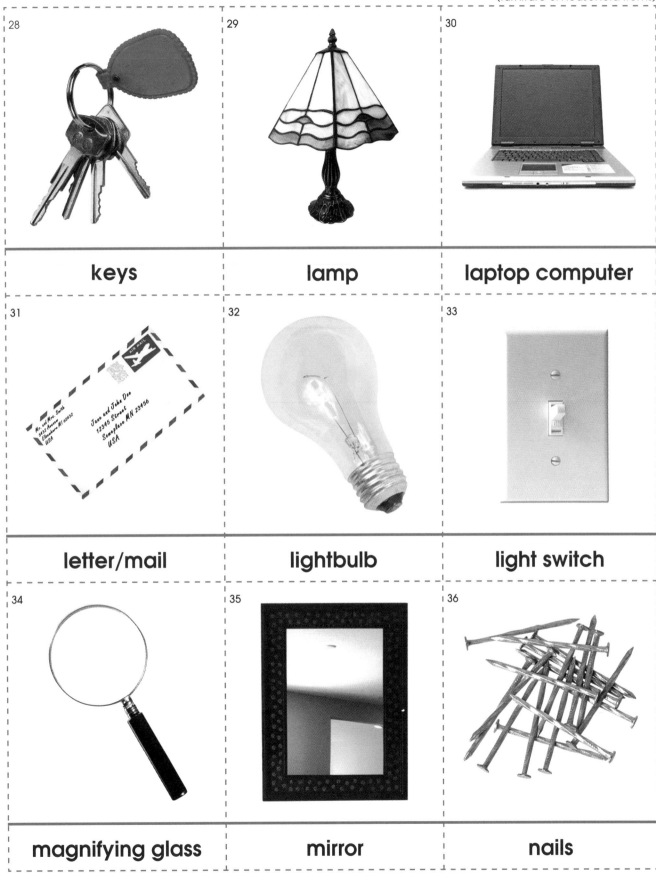

28	29	30
keys	lamp	laptop computer
31	32	33
letter/mail	lightbulb	light switch
34	35	36
magnifying glass	mirror	nails

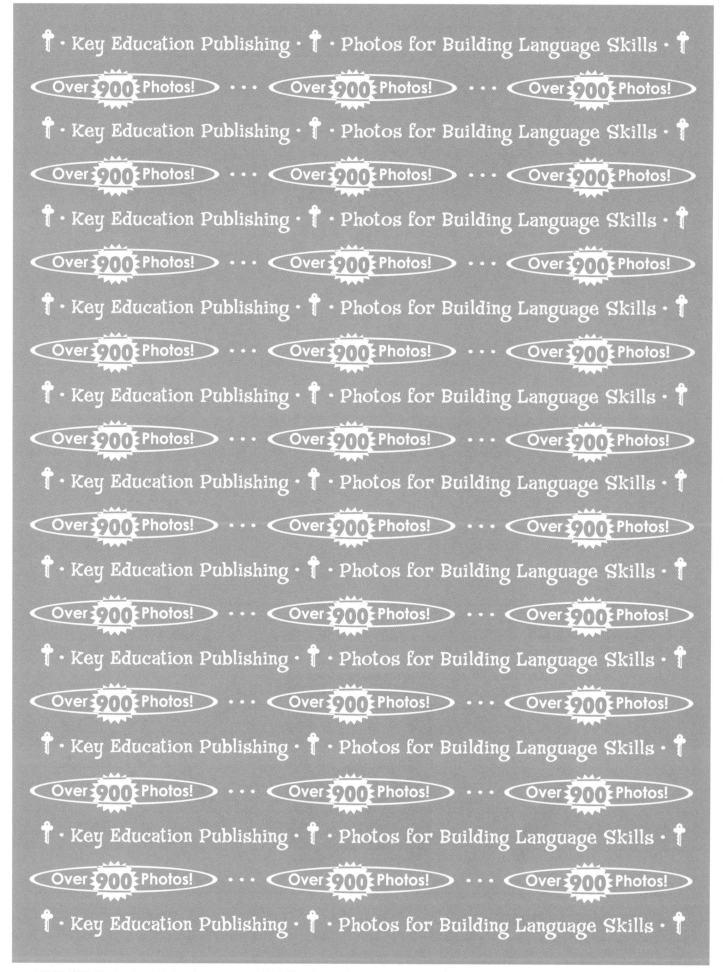

night stand	**pail**	**pens**
picnic basket	**picture (framed)**	**pillow**
rocking chair	**rug**	**sheets & blanket**

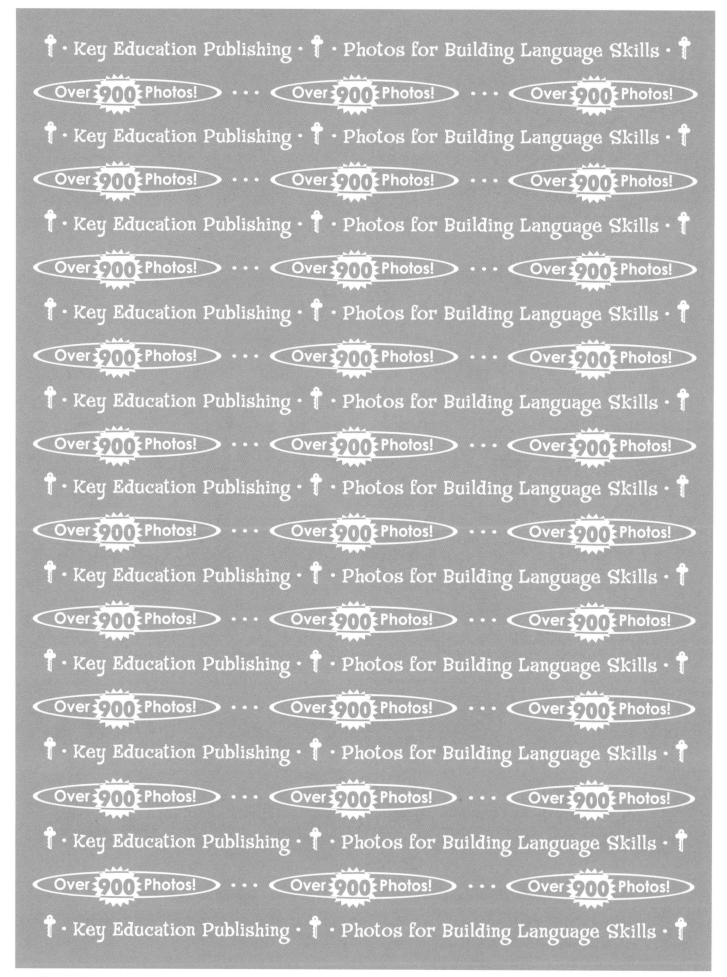

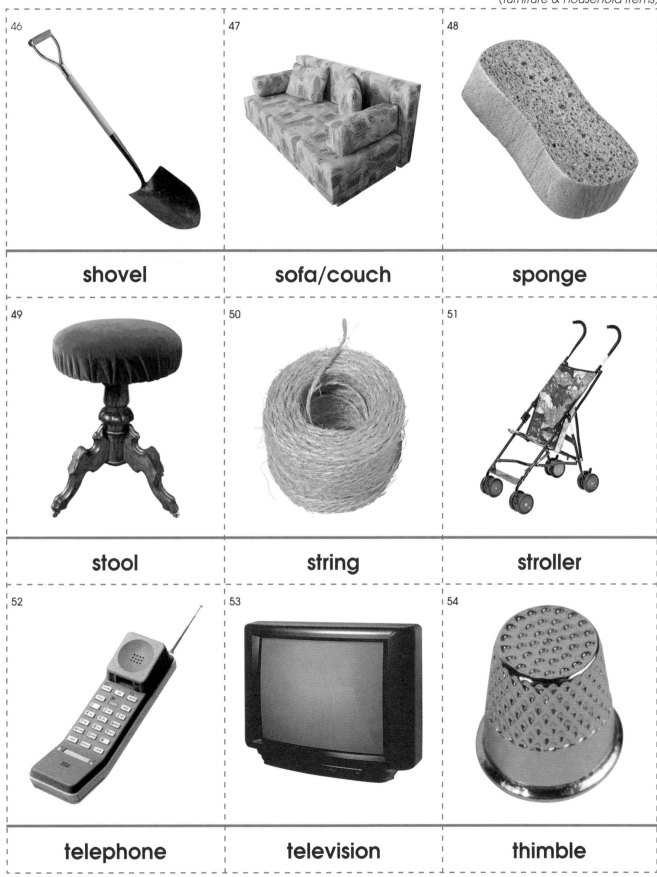

46 shovel

47 sofa/couch

48 sponge

49 stool

50 string

51 stroller

52 telephone

53 television

54 thimble

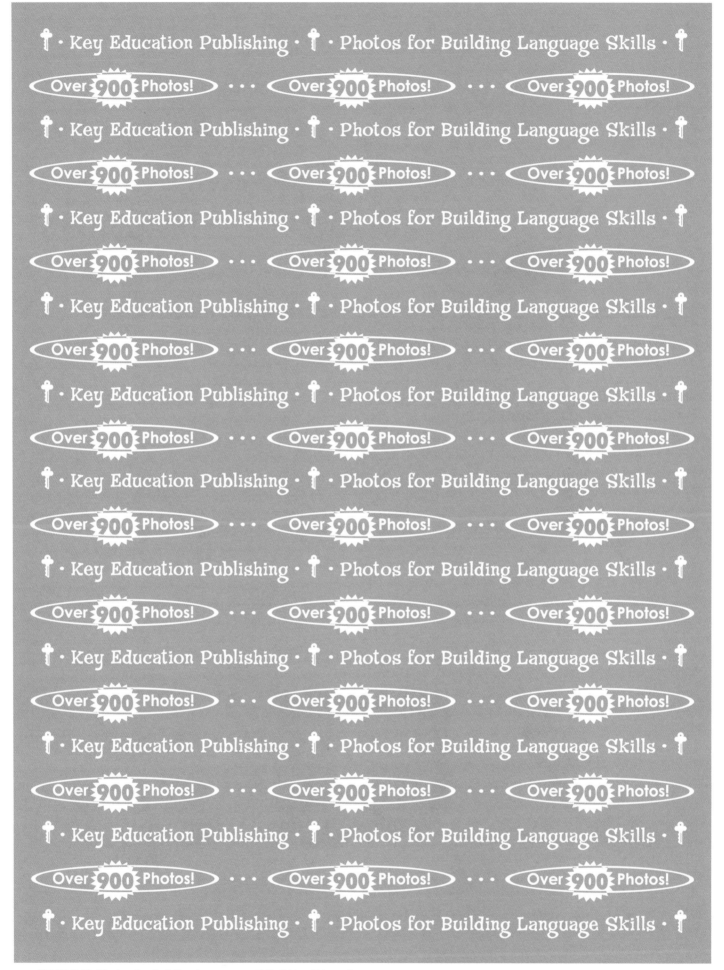

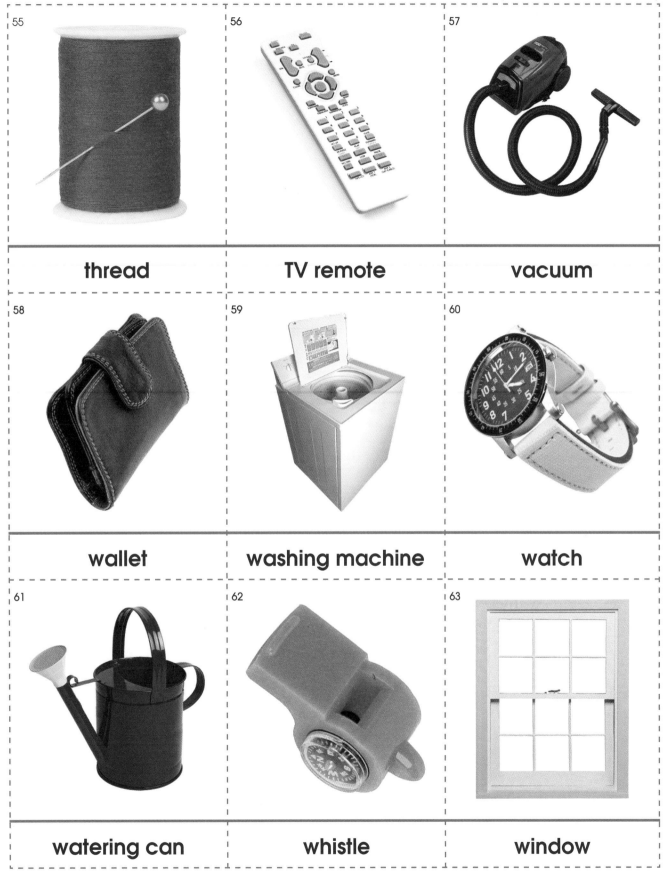

55 thread	56 TV remote	57 vacuum
58 wallet	59 washing machine	60 watch
61 watering can	62 whistle	63 window

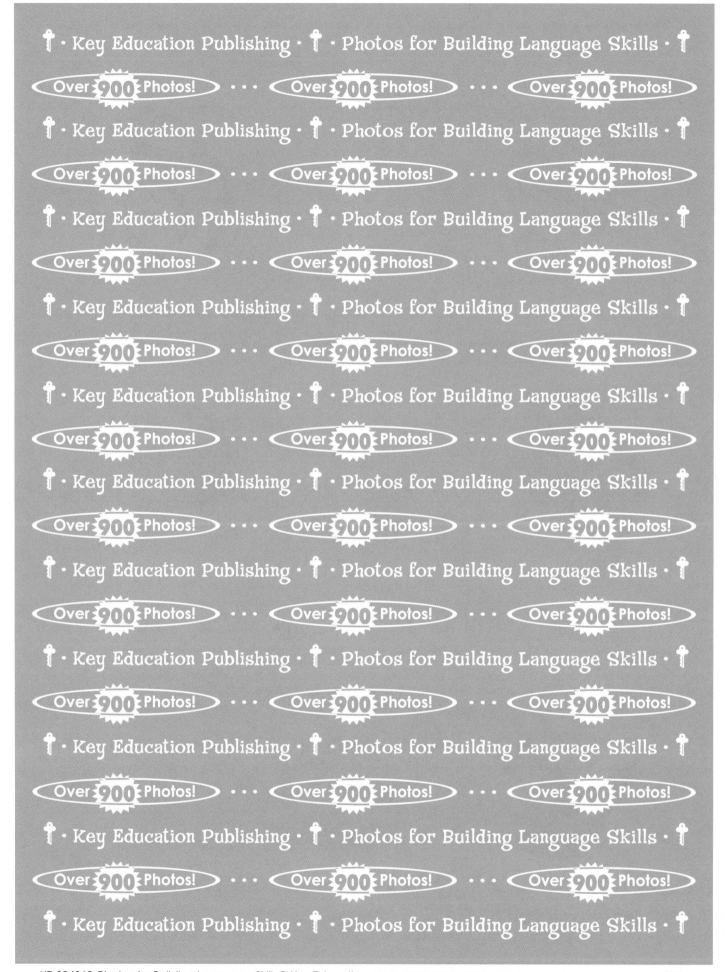

Chapter 10: Holidays & Seasons

birthday — cake	birthday — gifts	birthday — party things
Christmas — ornament	Christmas — tree	Christmas — Santa
Easter — bunny	Easter — eggs	4th of July — US flag

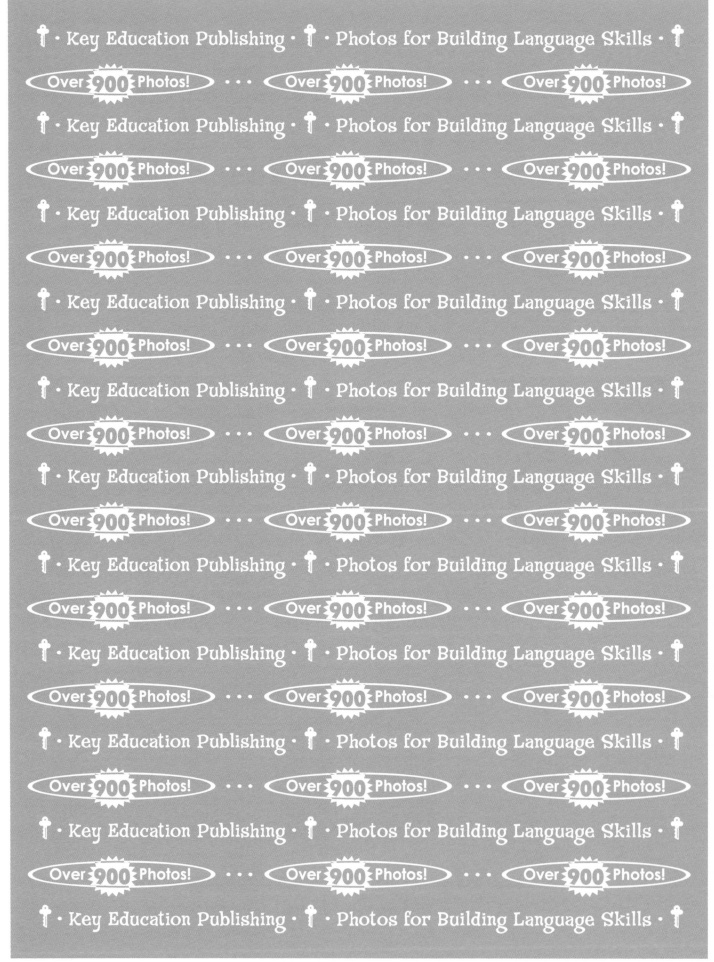

**4th of July —
fireworks**

**Halloween —
candy corn**

**Halloween —
costumes**

**Halloween —
pumpkins**

**Hanukkah —
dreidels**

**Hanukkah —
menorah**

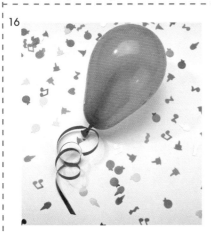

**special day —
balloon/confetti**

**special day —
balloons**

**St. Patrick's Day —
4-leaf clover**

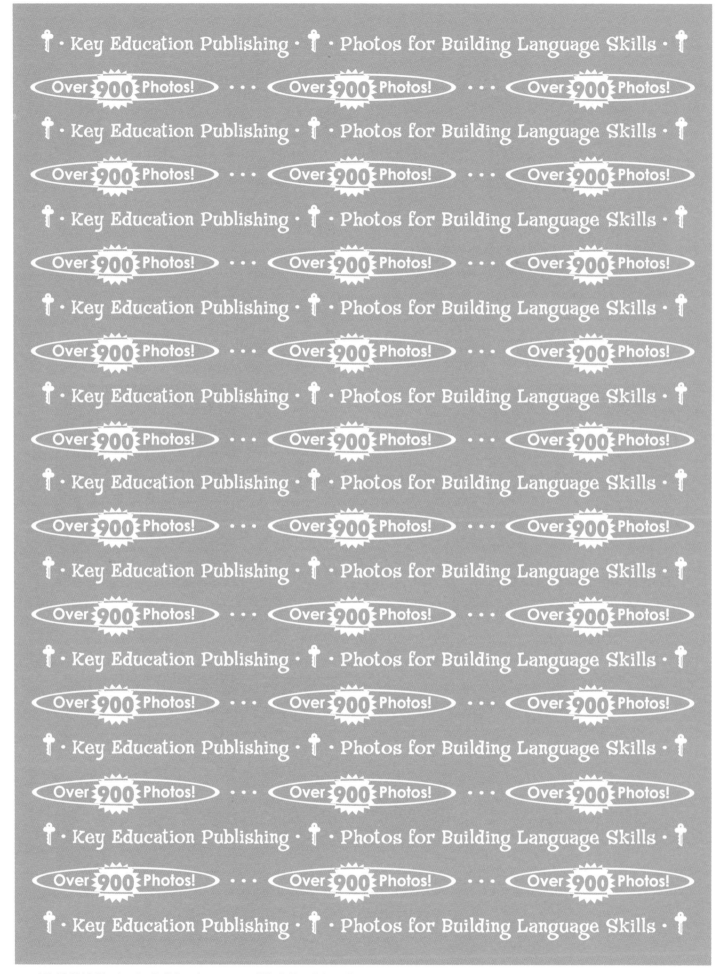

**Thanksgiving —
harvest**

**Thanksgiving —
turkey**

**Valentine's Day —
candy**

**Valentine's Day —
lollipops**

autumn — corn field

**autumn —
fun with leaves**

autumn — leaves

autumn — tree

spring — blossoms

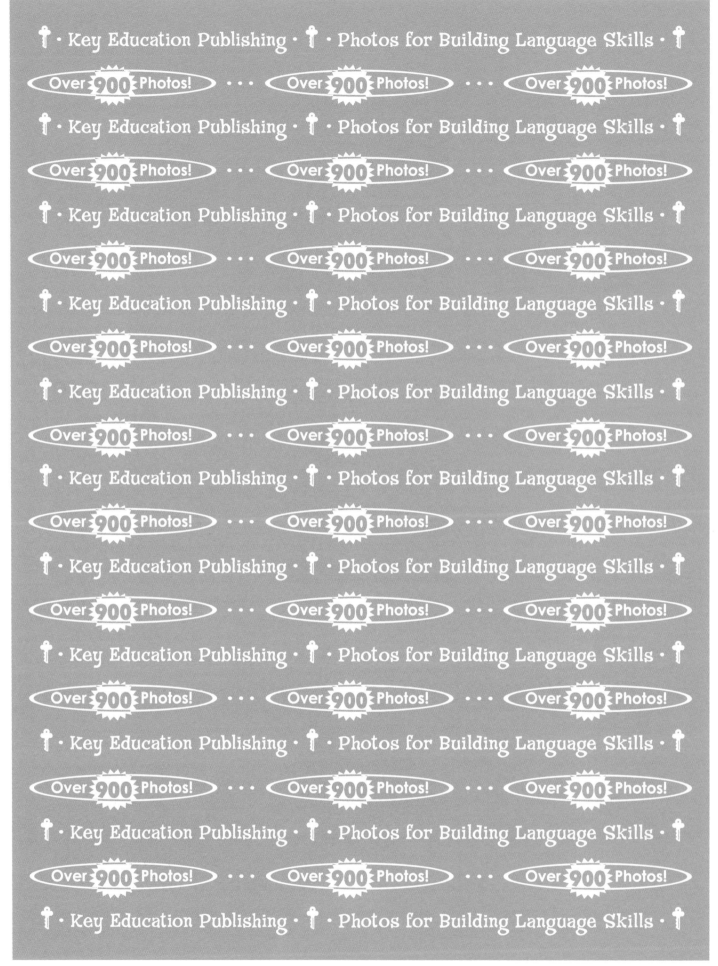

28

29

30

spring — flowers

spring — kite flying

summer — beach

31

32

33

summer — swimming pool

summer — water slide

winter — playing with the snow

34

35

36

winter — snowman

winter — sledding

winter — tree

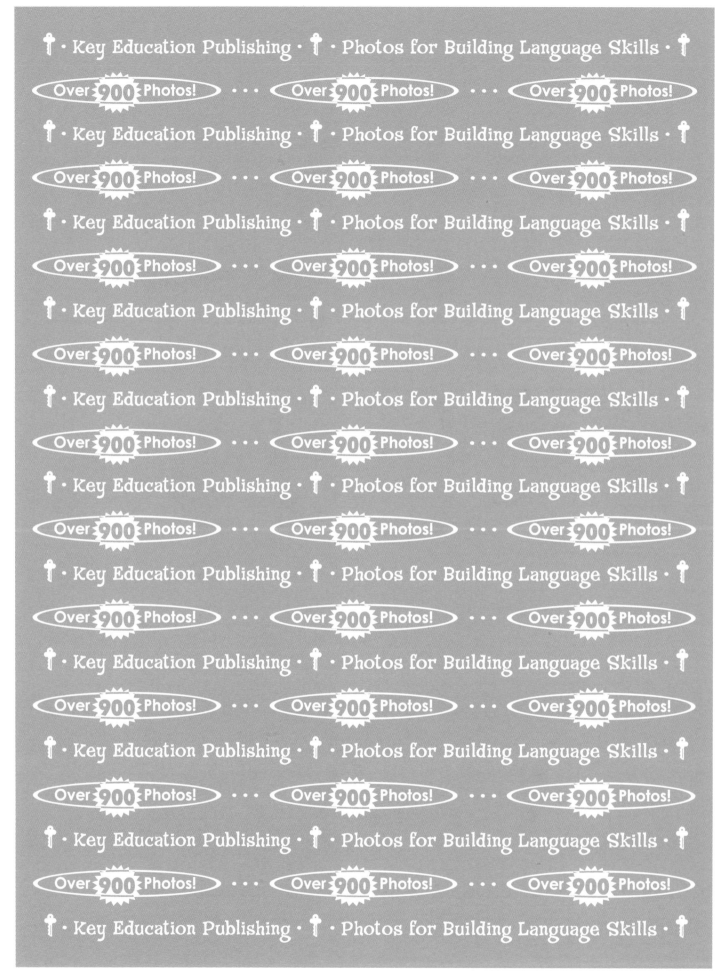

1 blender	2 bowls	3 coffee maker
4 cup	5 cutting board	6 dishwasher
7 dishwashing soap	8 electric frying pan	9 foil

10 fork	11 glass	12 ice cube tray
13 knife	14 measuring cups	15 measuring spoons
16 microwave	17 mixer	18 muffin tins

19	20	21
napkins	**oven mitt**	**paper towels**
22	23	24
placemats	**pan**	**plate**
25	26	27
refrigerator	**scoop**	**sink**

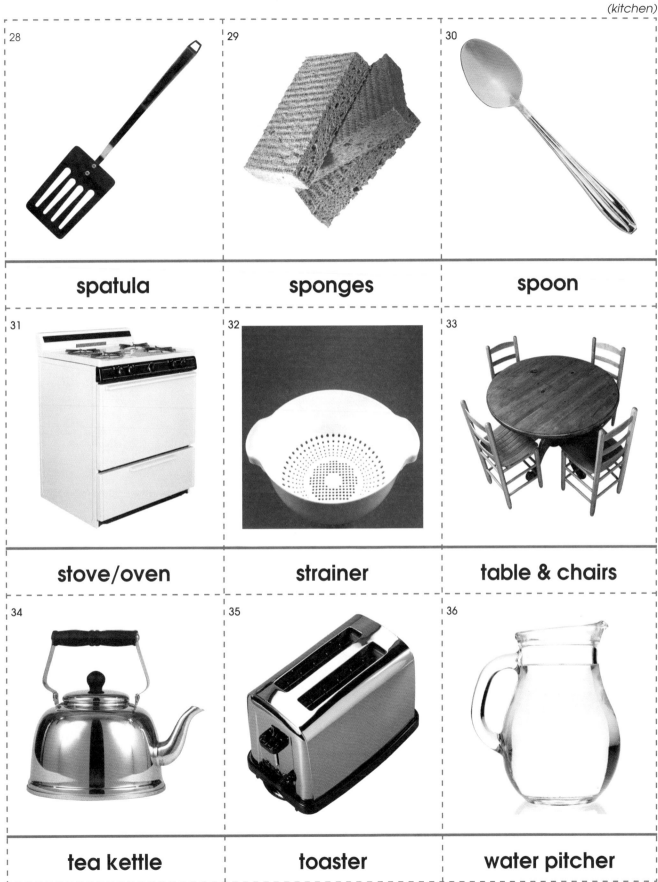

28	29	30
spatula	**sponges**	**spoon**
31	32	33
stove/oven	**strainer**	**table & chairs**
34	35	36
tea kettle	**toaster**	**water pitcher**

1 1¢ penny (front)

2 1¢ penny (back)

3 5¢ nickle (front)

4 5¢ nickle (back)

5 10¢ dime (front)

6 10¢ dime (back)

7 25¢ quarter (front)

8 25¢ quarter (back)

9 50¢ fifty-cent piece (front)

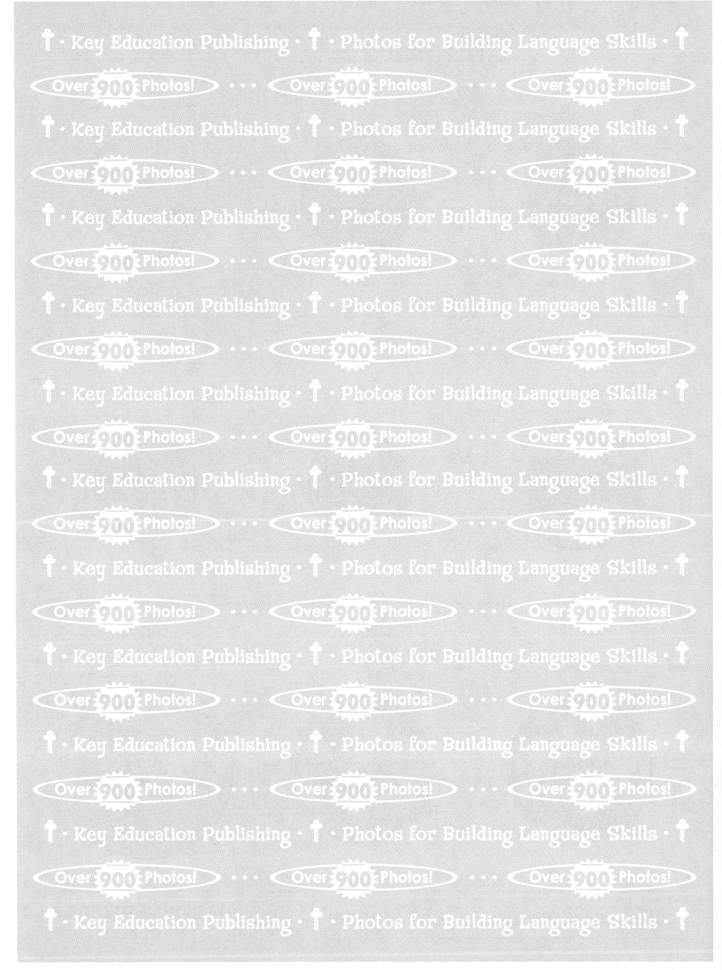

10

50¢ fifty-cent piece
(back)

11

1$ one dollar bill (front)

12

1$ one dollar bill (back)

13

5$ five dollar bill (front)

14

5$ five dollar bill (back)

15

10$ ten dollar bill (front)

16

10$ ten dollar bill (back)

17

20$ twenty dollar bill (front)

18

20$ twenty dollar bill (back)

Chapter 13: Music

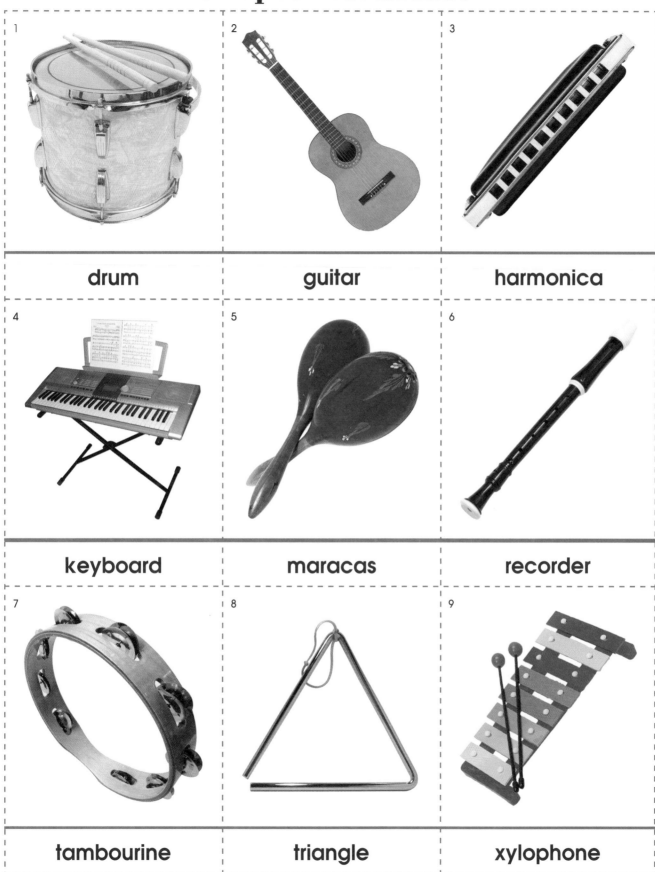

1 drum	2 guitar	3 harmonica
4 keyboard	5 maracas	6 recorder
7 tambourine	8 triangle	9 xylophone

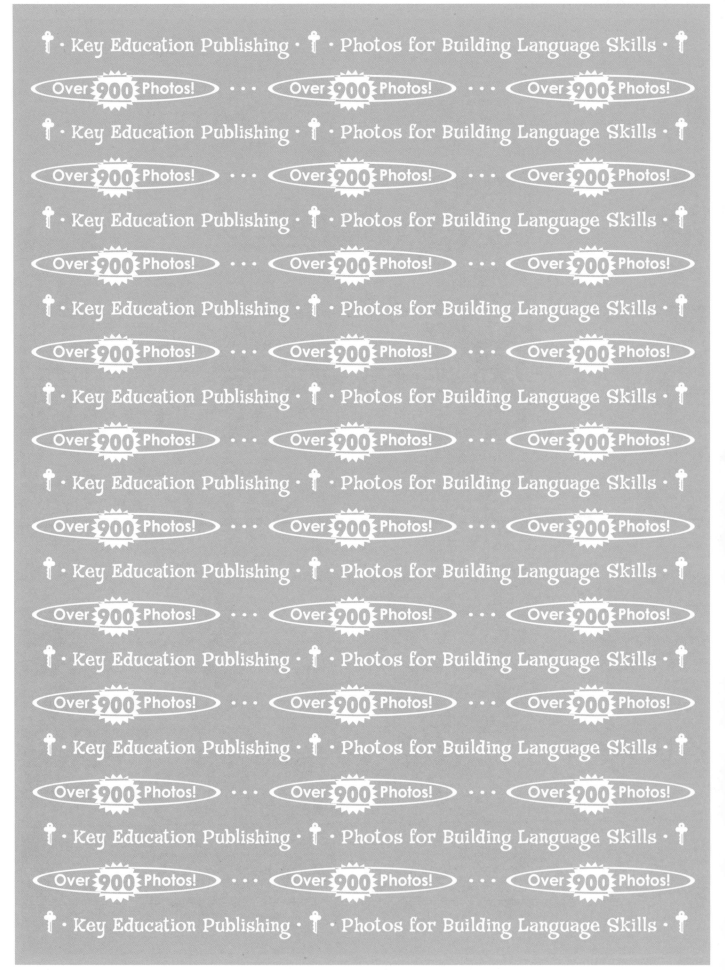

Chapter 14: Nature & Weather

acorns	beach	bird nest
clouds	dandelion	desert
fence & field	fog	flower

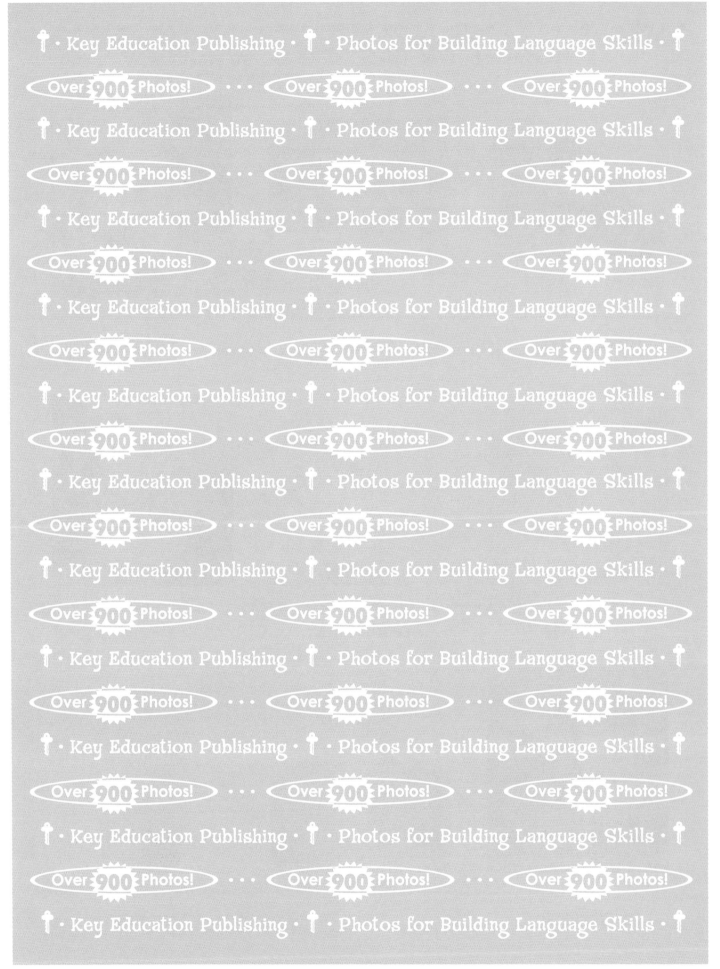

flower garden	footprints/sand	forest
grass	lake	lightning
moon	mountain	pinecone

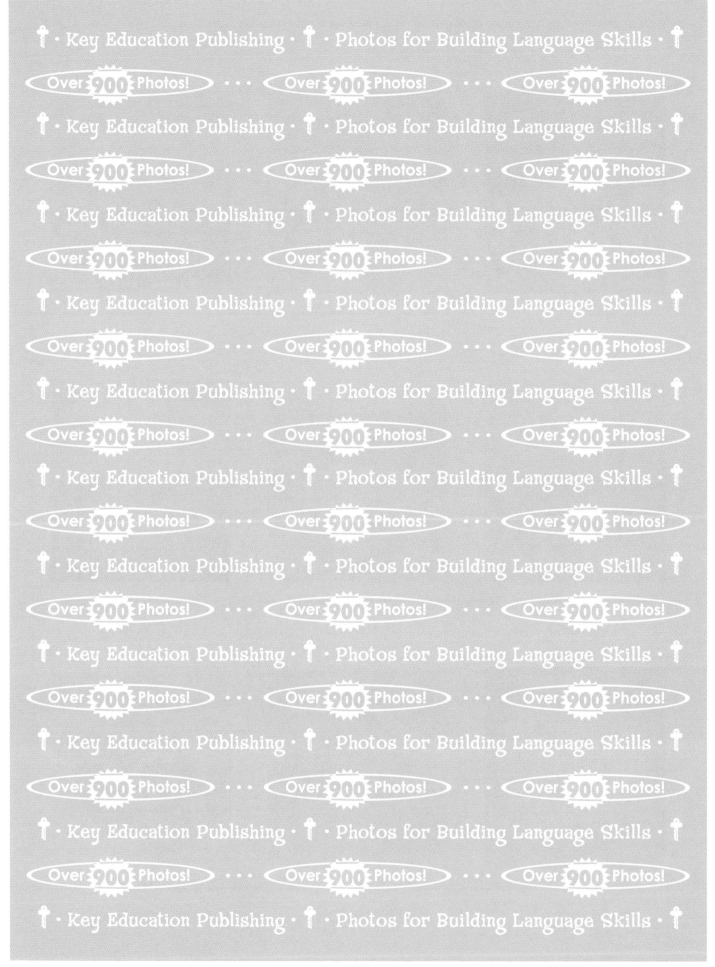

19	20	21
rain	**rainbow**	**rain clothes**
22	23	24
river	**rocks**	**seashells**
25	26	27
snow storm	**squirrel**	**stars**

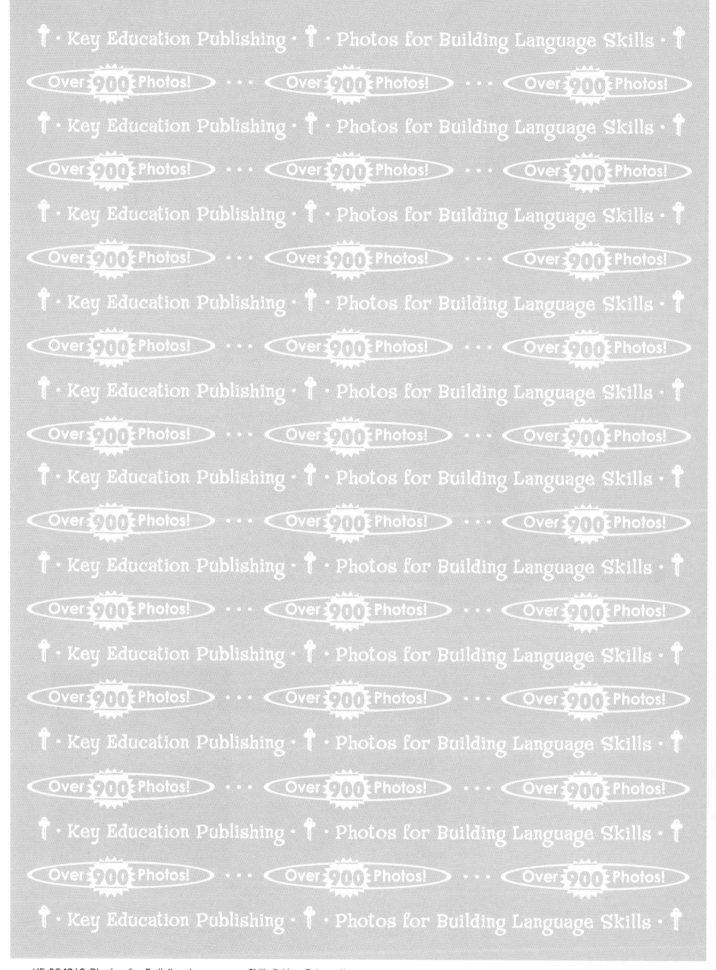

28	29	30
storm clouds	**sun**	**sunrise**
31	32	33
sunset	**tornado**	**tree**
34	35	36
vegetable garden	**waterfall**	**windy**

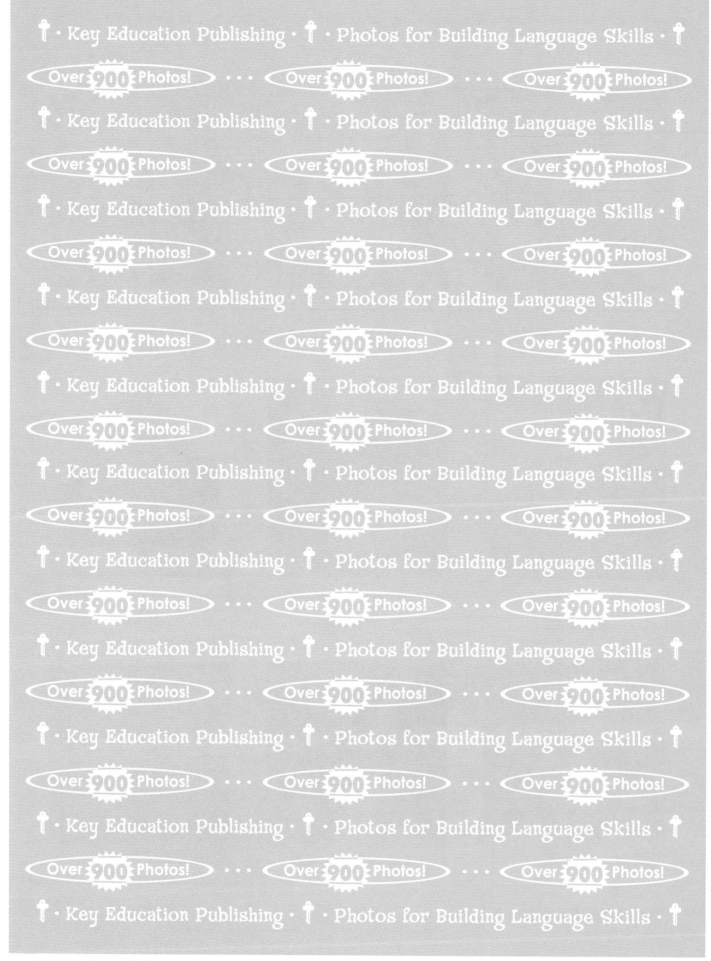

KE-804062 *Photos for Building Language Skills* © Key Education

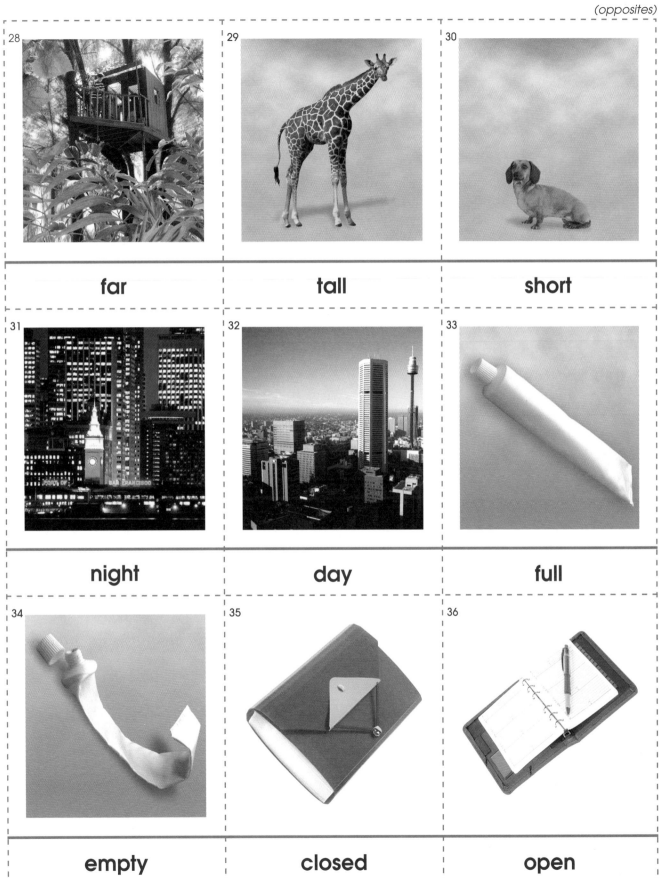

28 far

29 tall

30 short

31 night

32 day

33 full

34 empty

35 closed

36 open

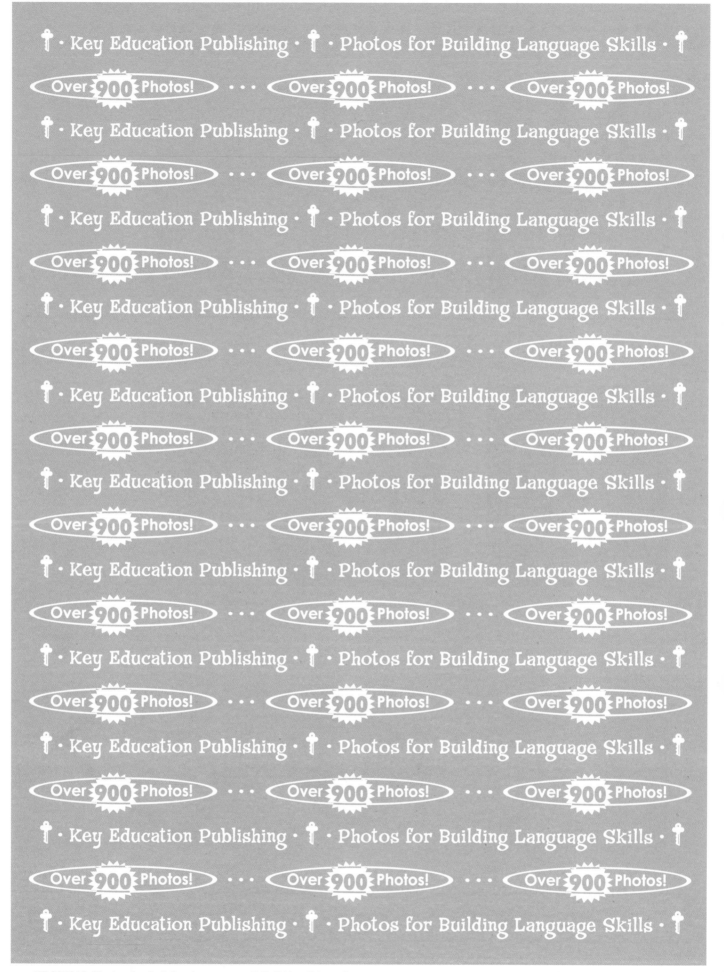

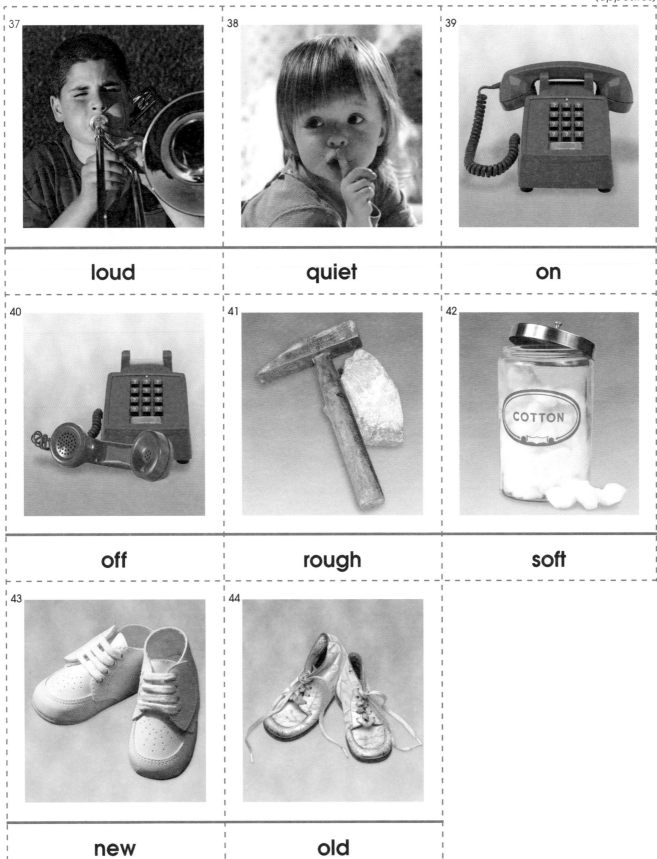

37 loud

38 quiet

39 on

40 off

41 rough

42 soft

43 new

44 old

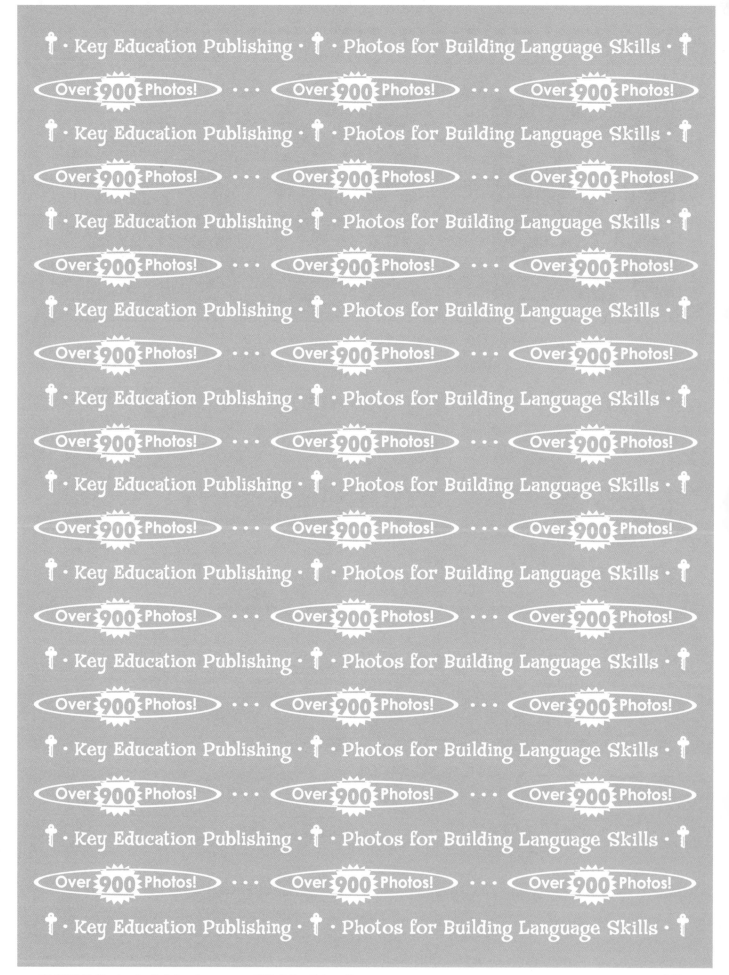

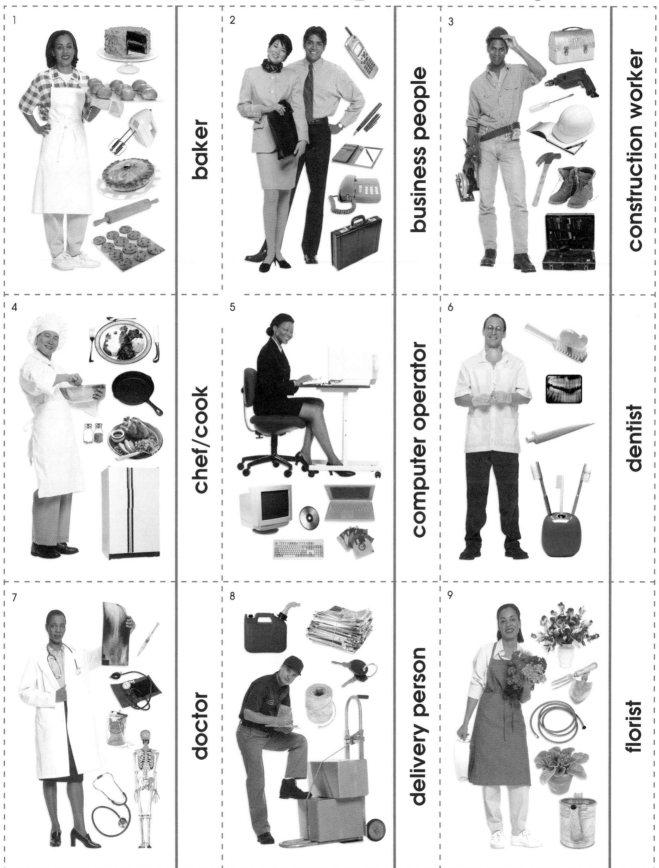

1. baker
2. business people
3. construction worker
4. chef/cook
5. computer operator
6. dentist
7. doctor
8. delivery person
9. florist

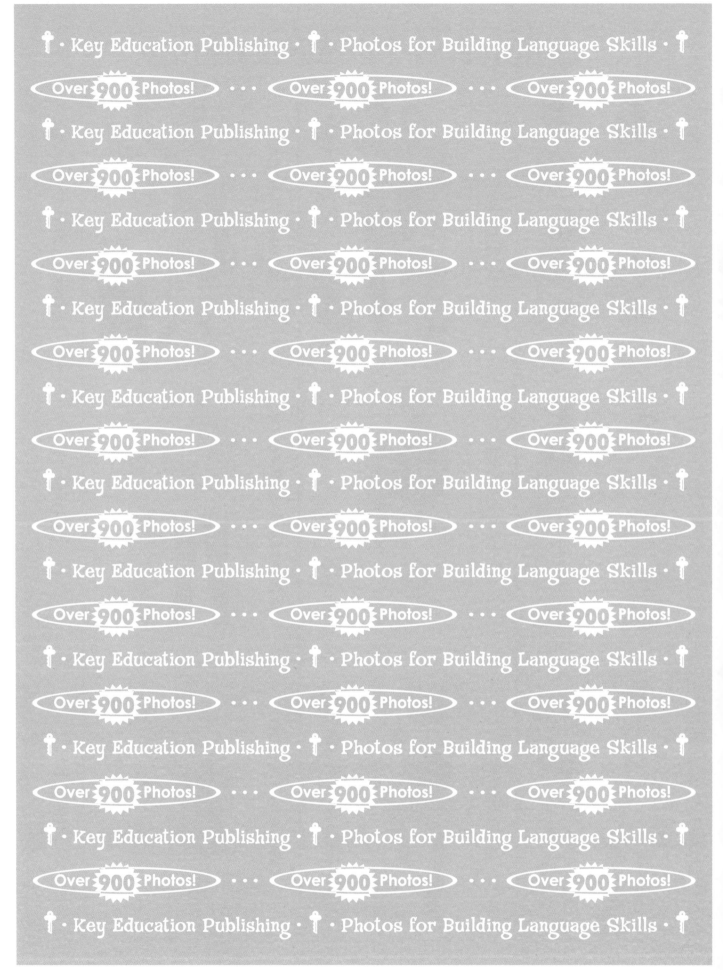

10   **fire fighter**

11   **grocer**

12   **janitor**

13   **librarian**

14   **mail carrier**

15   **nurse**

16   **painter**

17   **police officer**

18   **pilot/flight attendant**

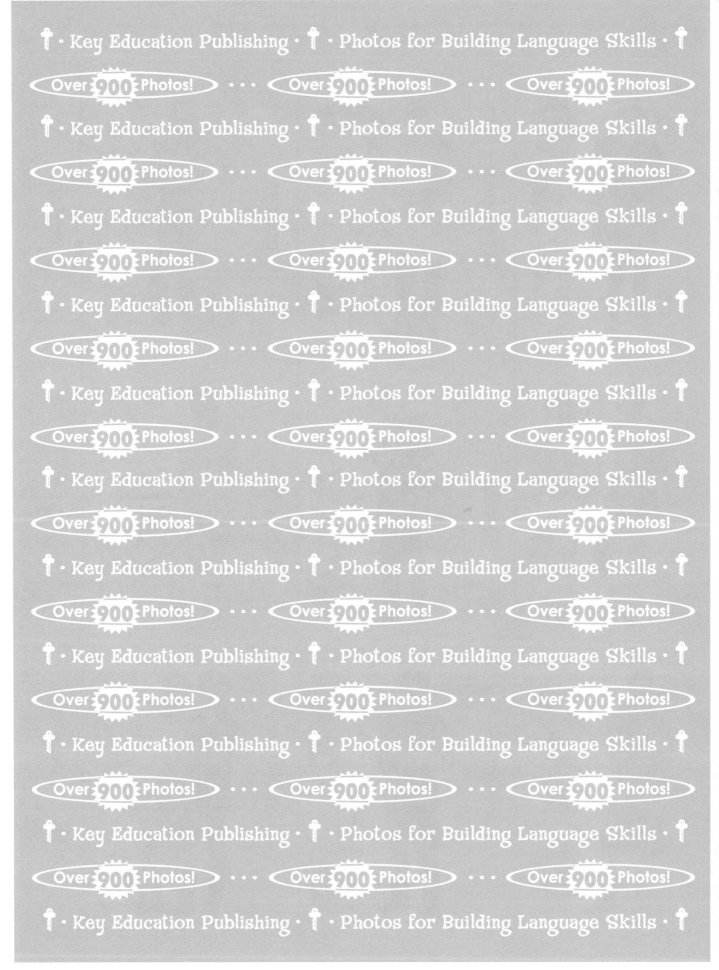

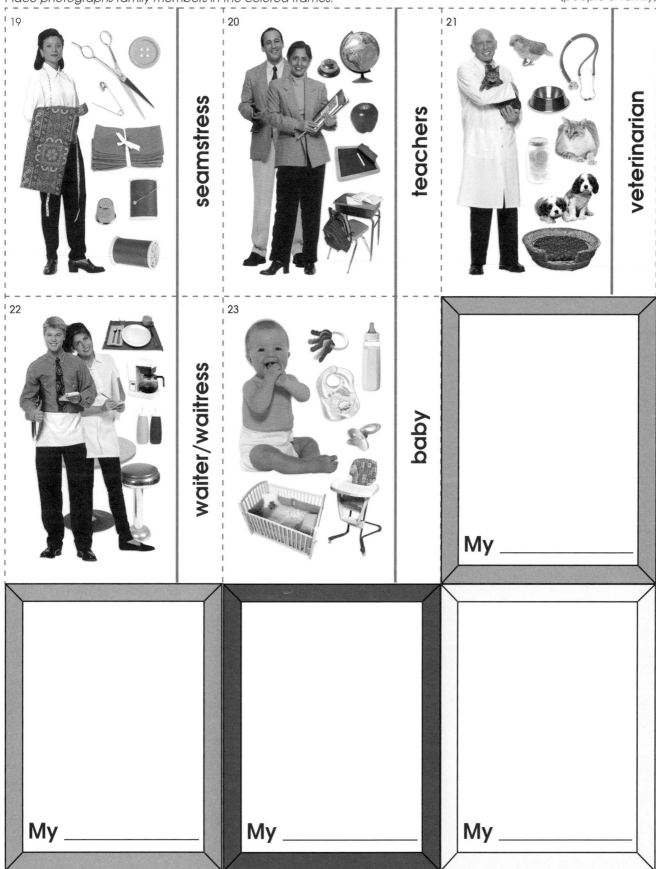

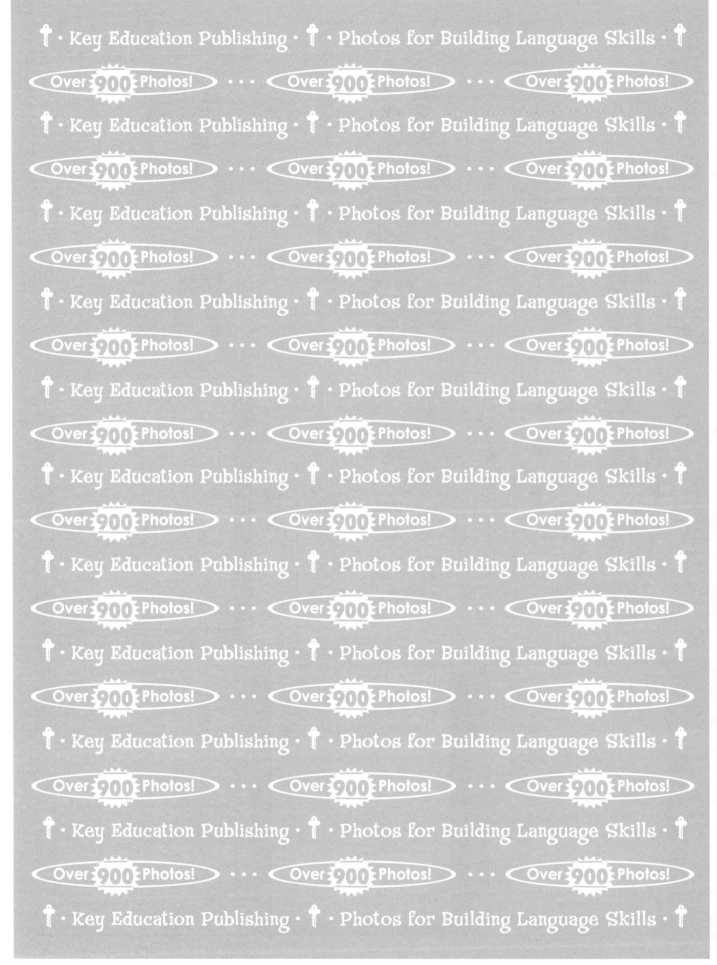

Tape photographs of family members in the colored frames. *(people & family)*

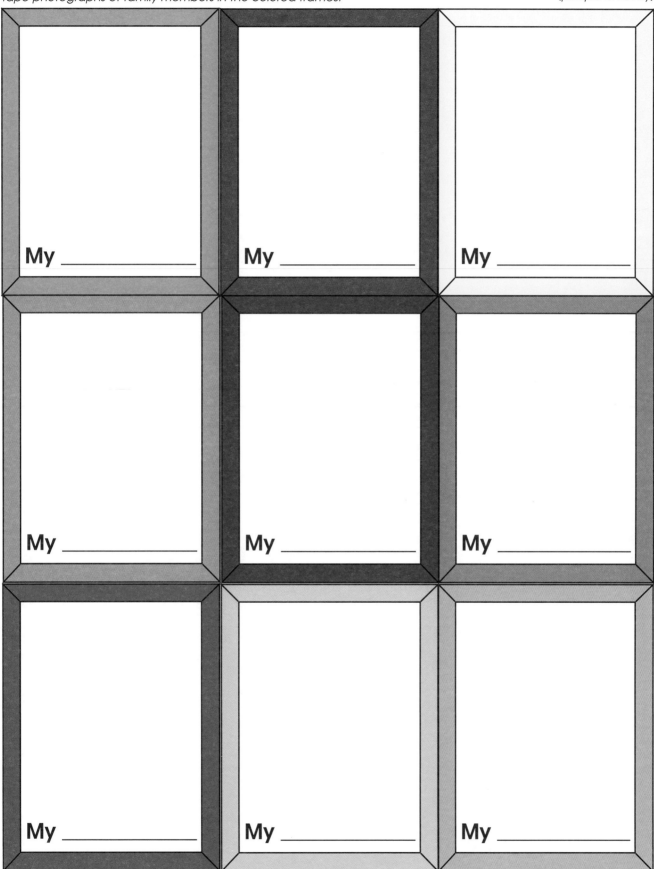

My _____

My _____

My _____

My _____

My _____

My _____

My _____

My _____

My _____

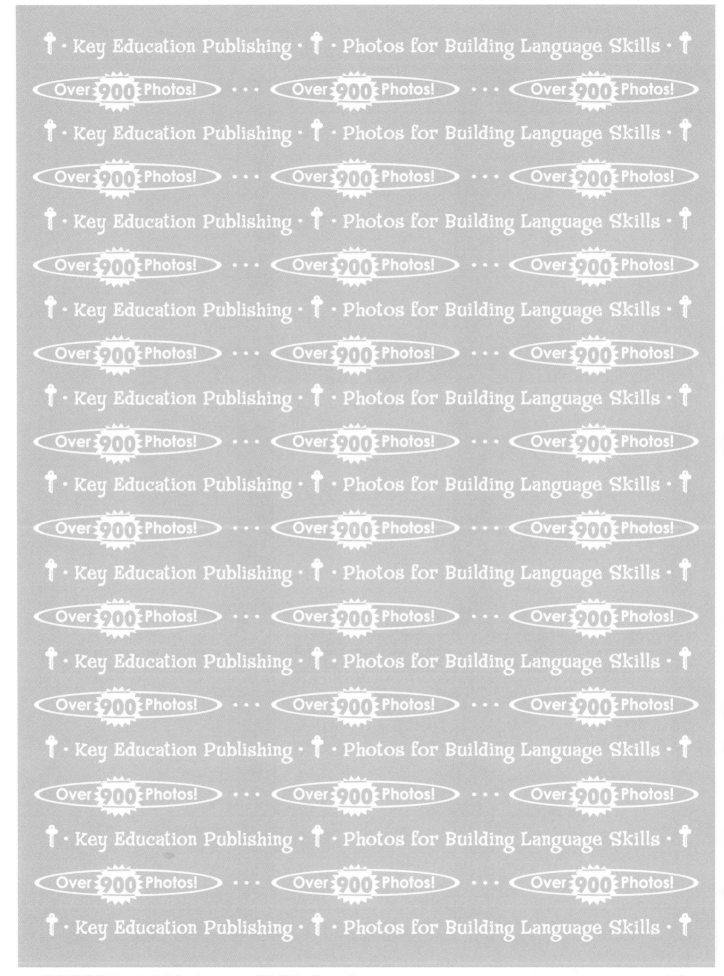

classroom — elementary

classroom — preschool

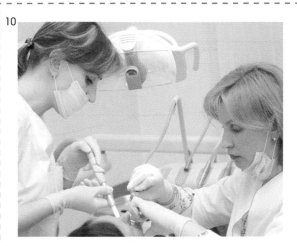

clothing store

dental office

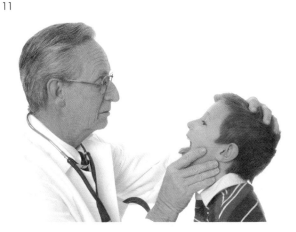

doctor's office

doctor's office/ getting a shot

backyard

bathroom

bedroom

child's bedroom

computer/home office

dining room

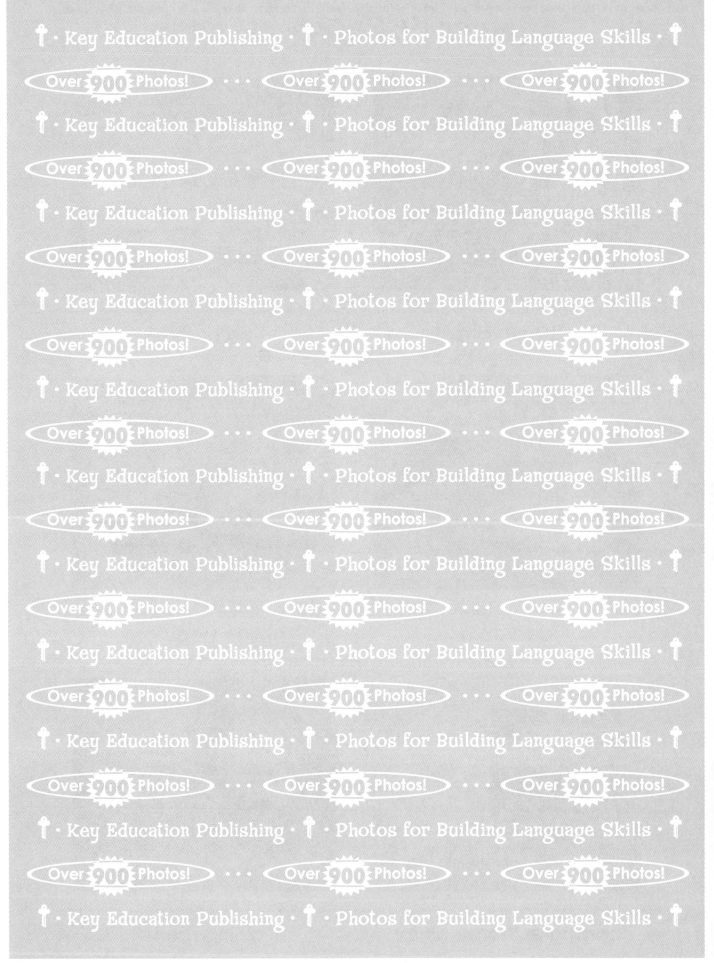

7

family/TV room

8

garage

9

kitchen

10

laundry room

11

living room

12

playroom

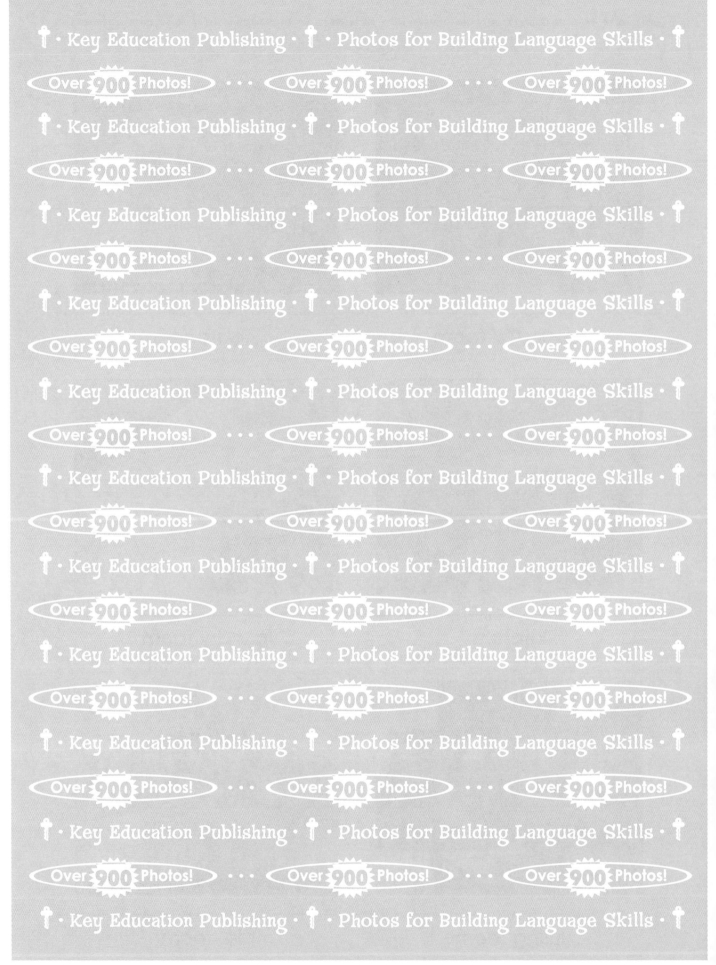

Chapter 20: School Tools

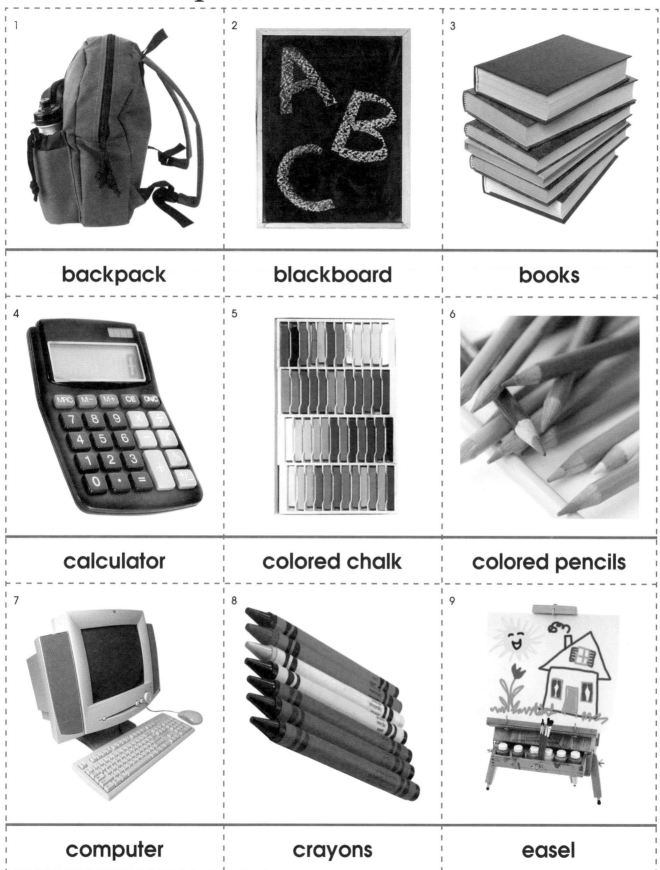

1 backpack	2 blackboard	3 books
4 calculator	5 colored chalk	6 colored pencils
7 computer	8 crayons	9 easel

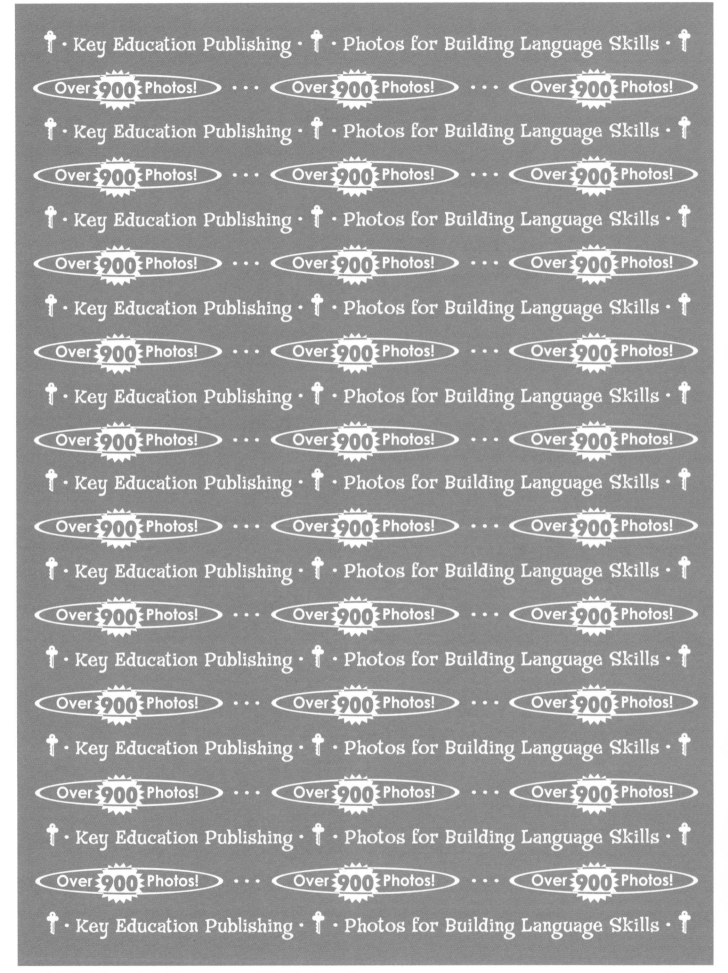

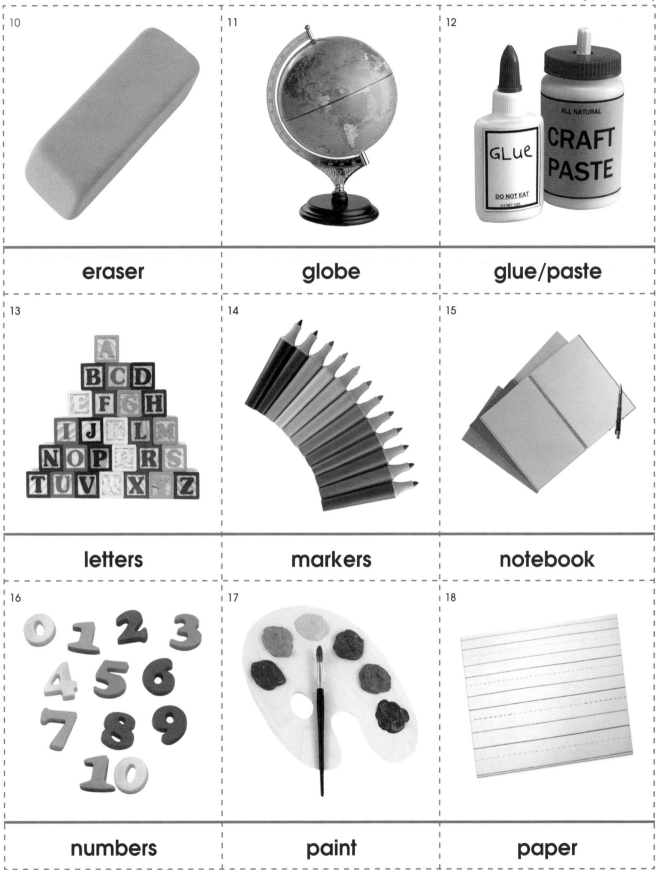

10	11	12
eraser	**globe**	**glue/paste**
13	14	15
letters	**markers**	**notebook**
16	17	18
numbers	**paint**	**paper**

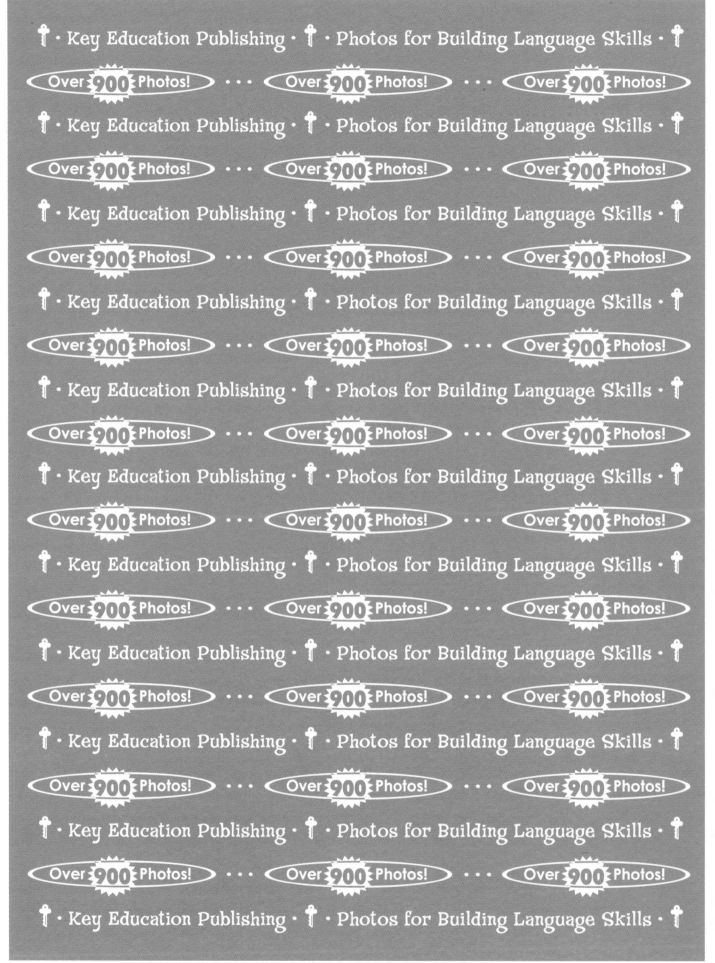

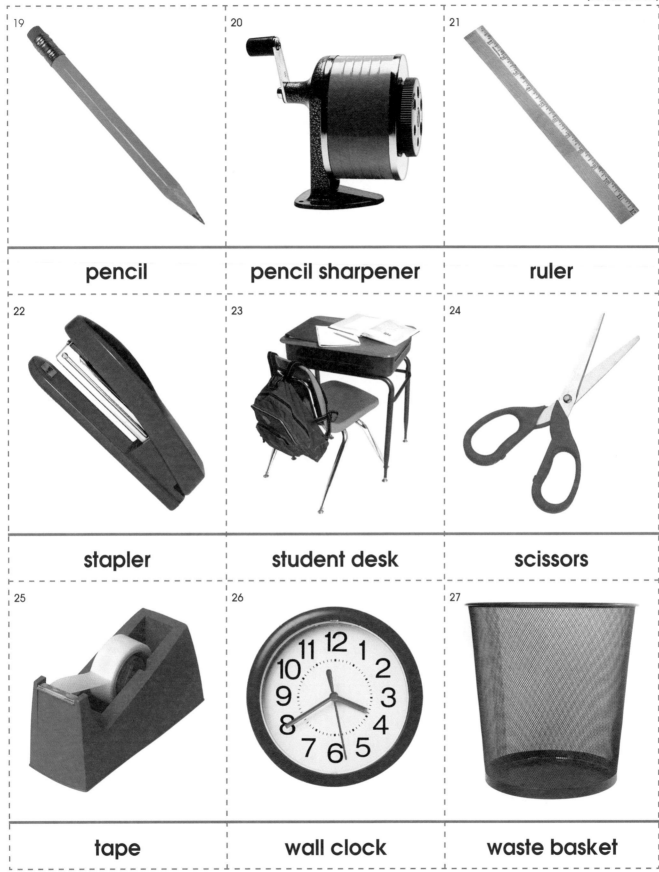

19 **pencil**	20 **pencil sharpener**	21 **ruler**
22 **stapler**	23 **student desk**	24 **scissors**
25 **tape**	26 **wall clock**	27 **waste basket**

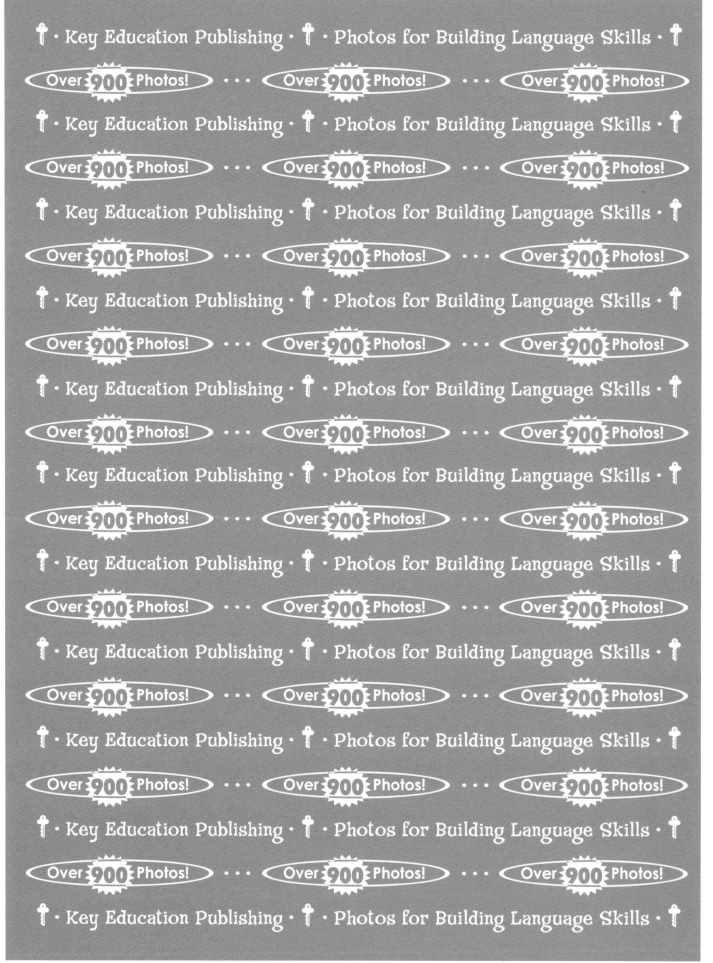

1 cat

2 come

3 dog

4 drink

5 eat

6 friend

7 **funny**

8 **go**

9 **good**

10 **happy**

11 **I love you**

12 **I/me**

13	14
like	listen
15	16
mad	more
17	18
please	sad

19 sick

20 sorry

21 stop

22 thank you

23 tired

24 toilet

25 **want**

26 **wash**

27 **water**

28 **What's wrong**

29 **yes**

30 **you**

(time on the hour)

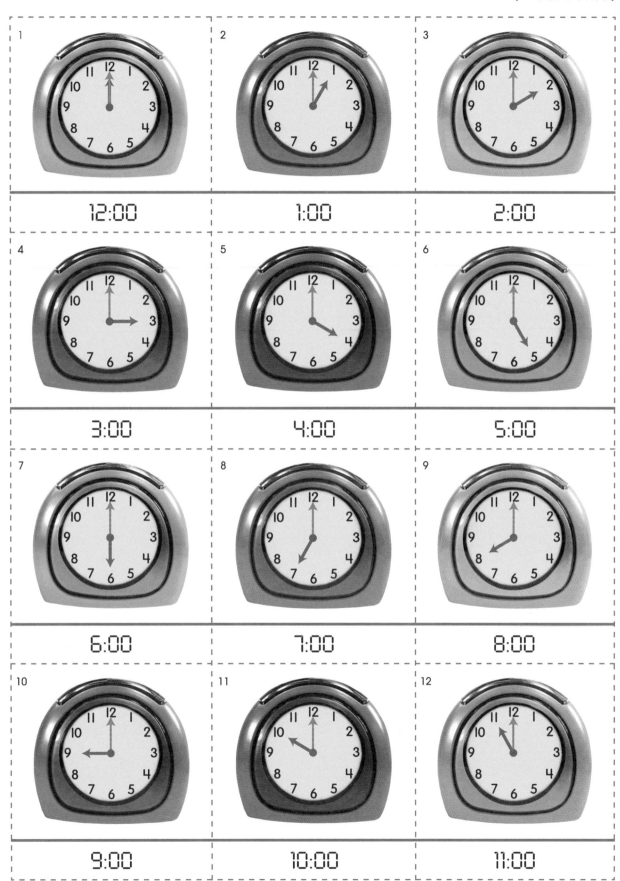

1	**2**	**3**
12:00	1:00	2:00
4	**5**	**6**
3:00	4:00	5:00
7	**8**	**9**
6:00	7:00	8:00
10	**11**	**12**
9:00	10:00	11:00

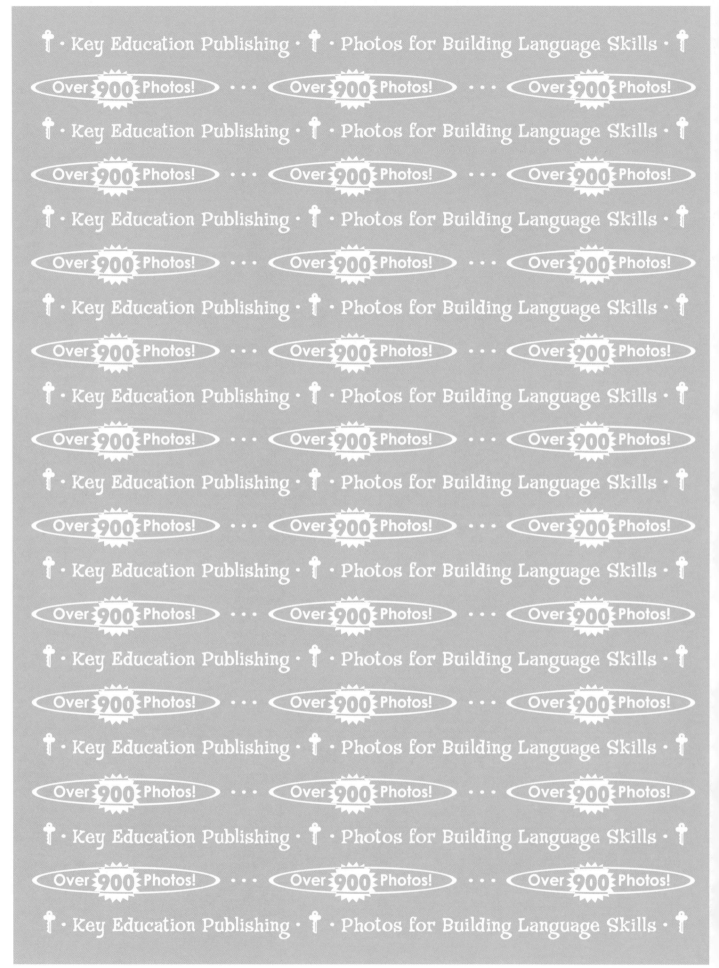

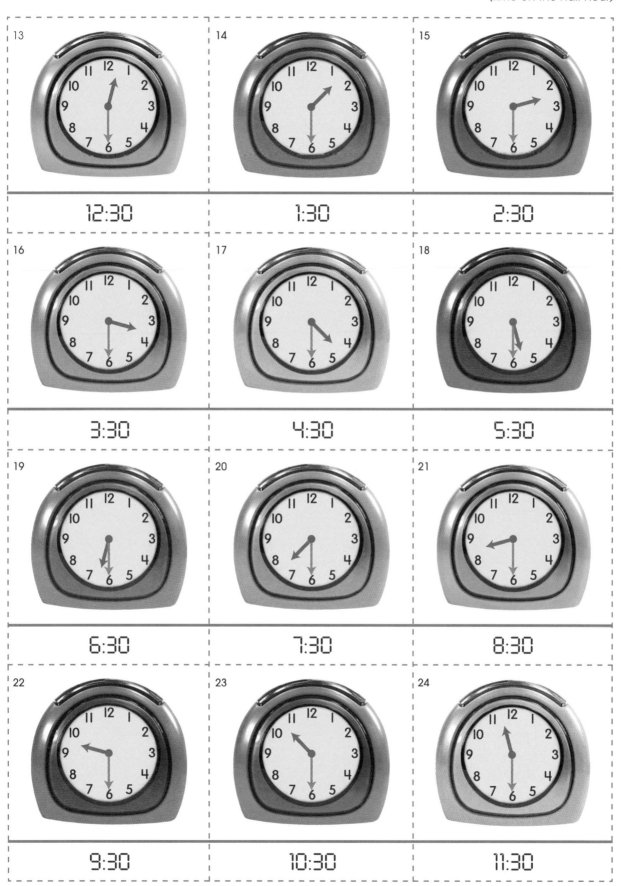

13	14	15
12:30	1:30	2:30
16	17	18
3:30	4:30	5:30
19	20	21
6:30	7:30	8:30
22	23	24
9:30	10:30	11:30

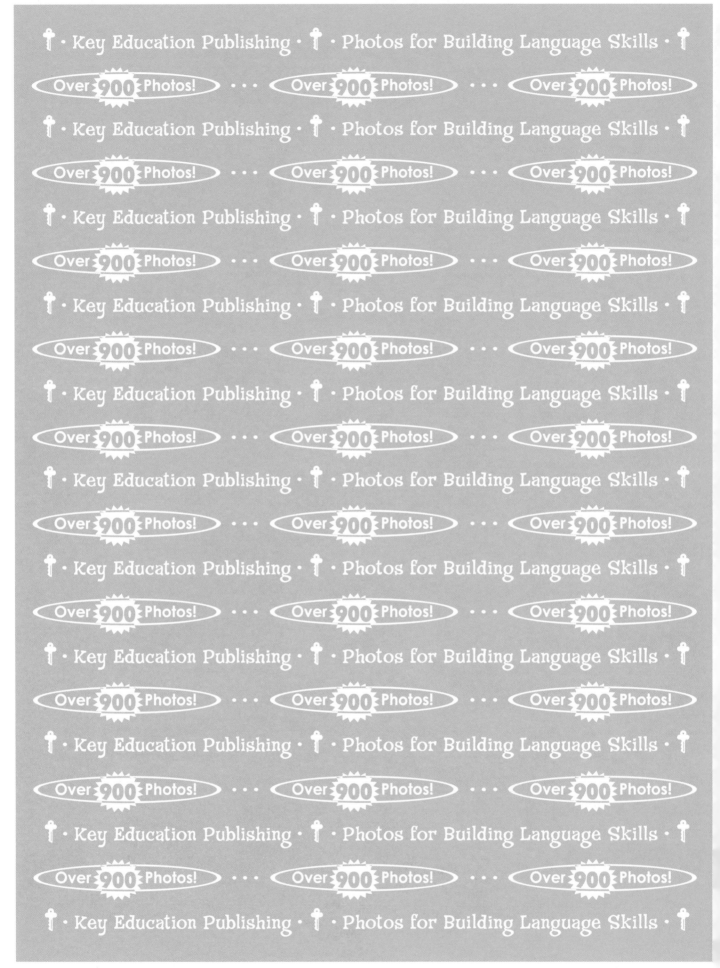

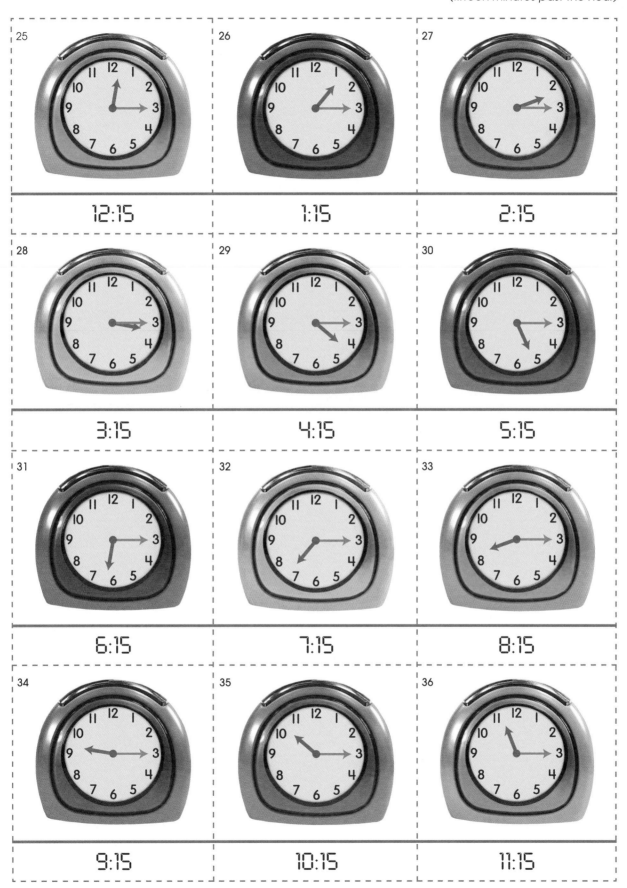

25 — 12:15	26 — 1:15	27 — 2:15
28 — 3:15	29 — 4:15	30 — 5:15
31 — 6:15	32 — 7:15	33 — 8:15
34 — 9:15	35 — 10:15	36 — 11:15

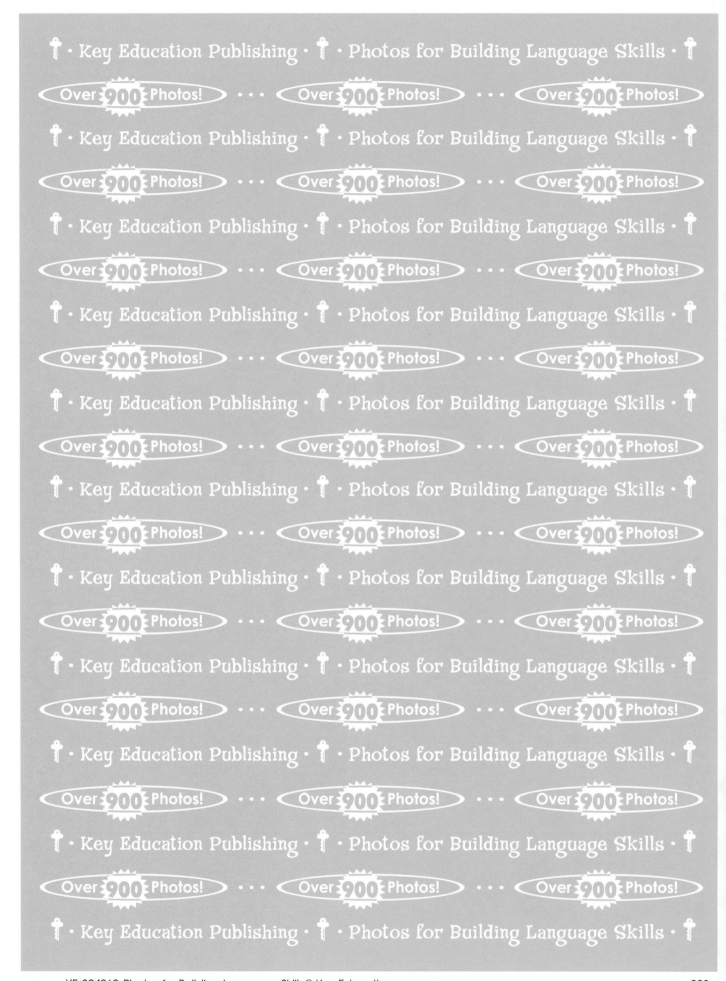

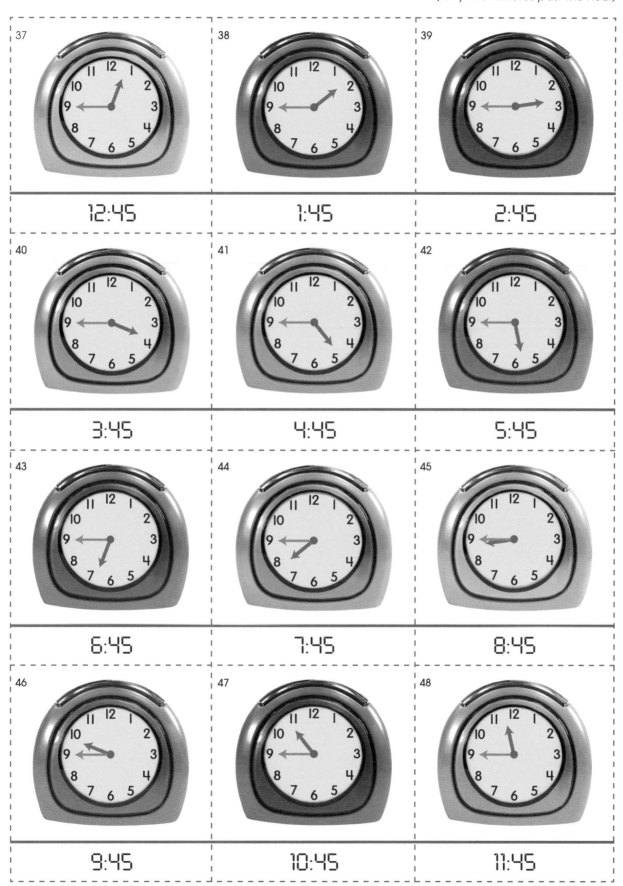

37	38	39
12:45	1:45	2:45
40	41	42
3:45	4:45	5:45
43	44	45
6:45	7:45	8:45
46	47	48
9:45	10:45	11:45

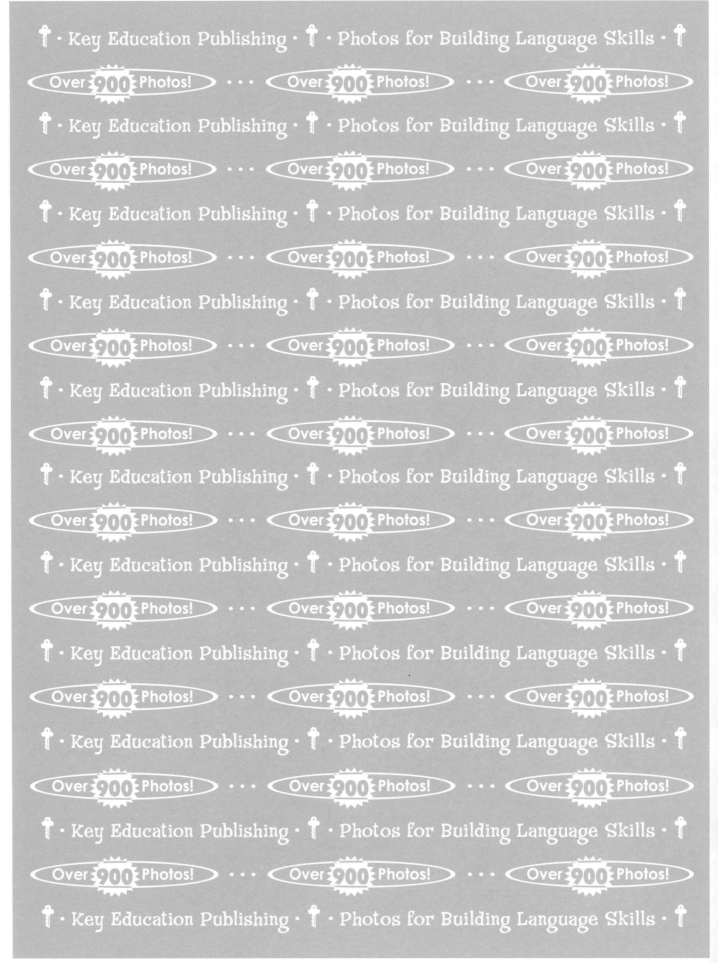

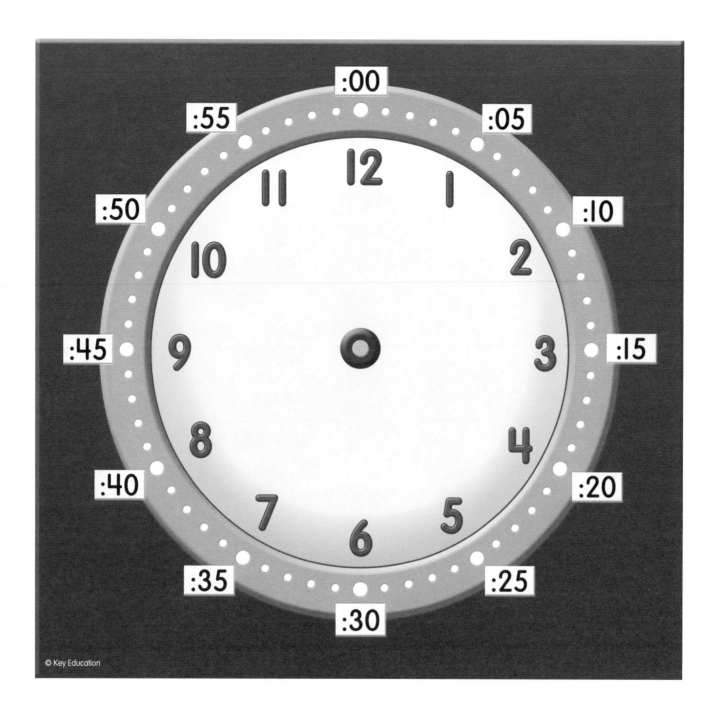

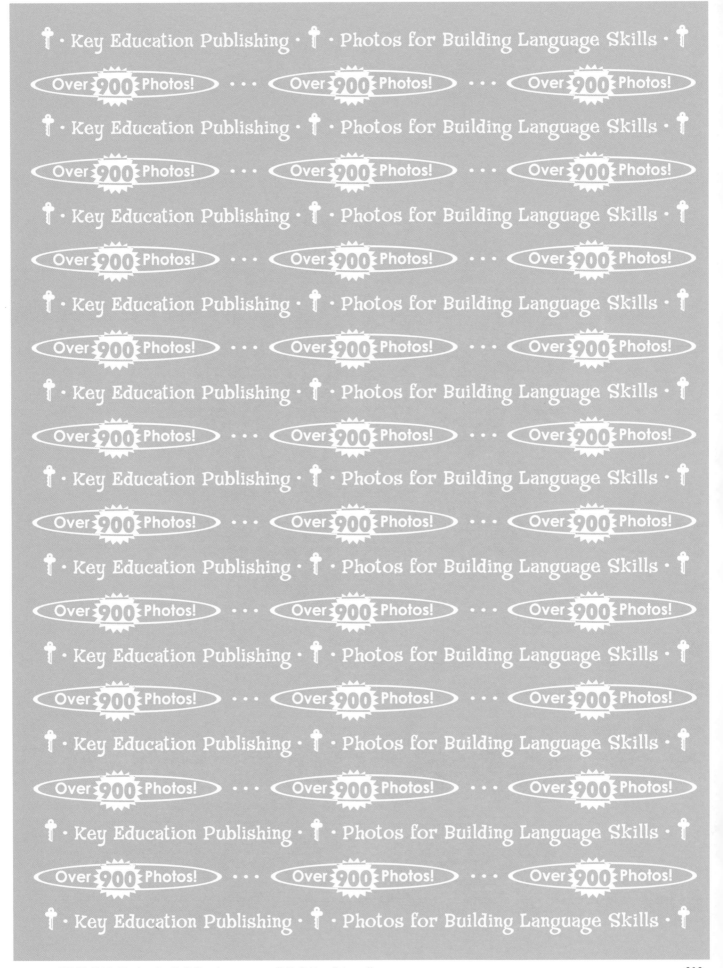

Chapter 24: Toys

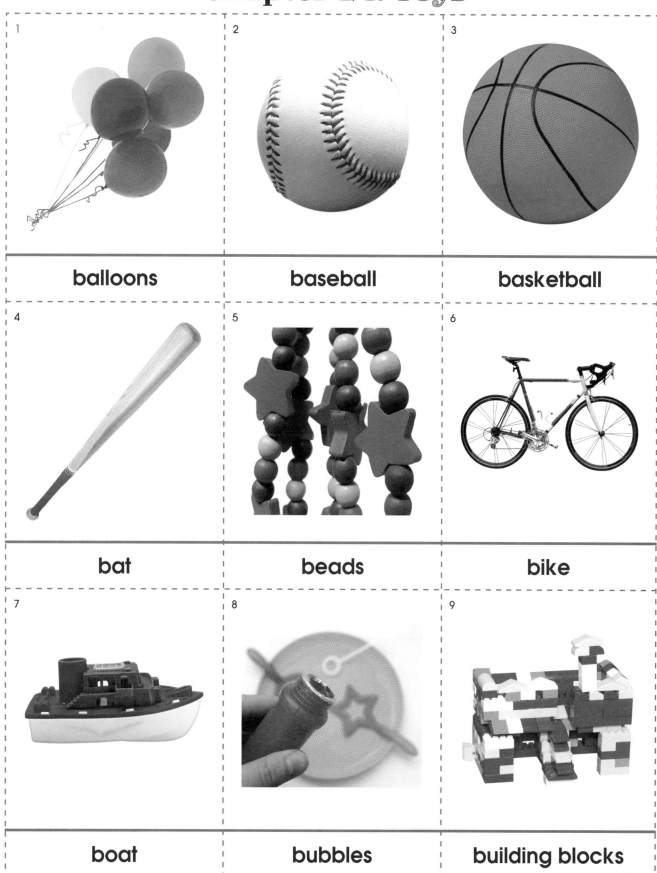

1 balloons	2 baseball	3 basketball
4 bat	5 beads	6 bike
7 boat	8 bubbles	9 building blocks

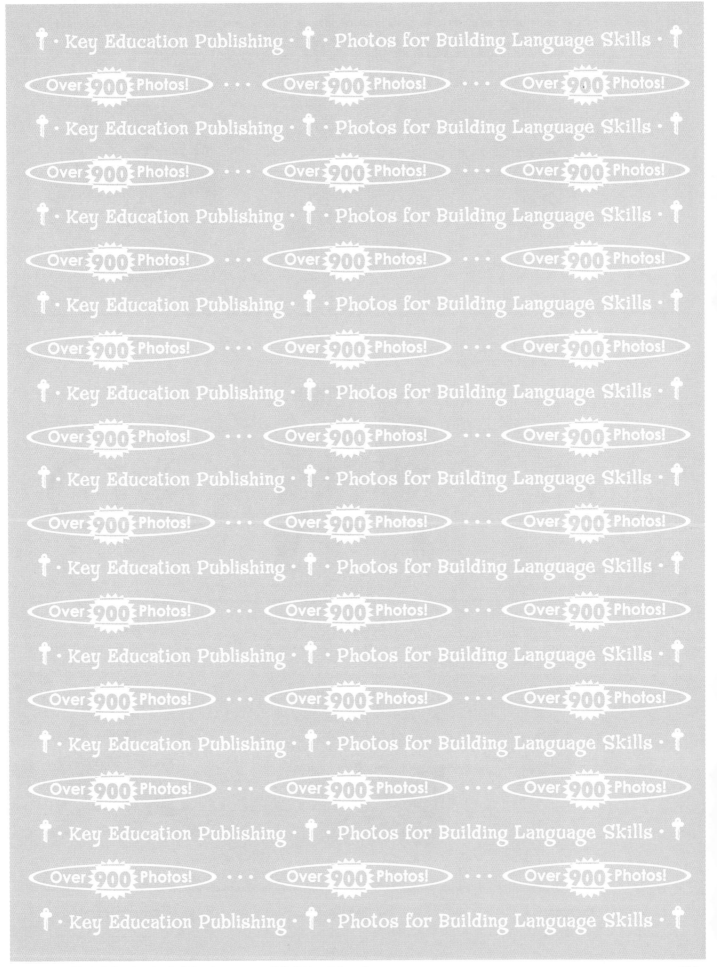

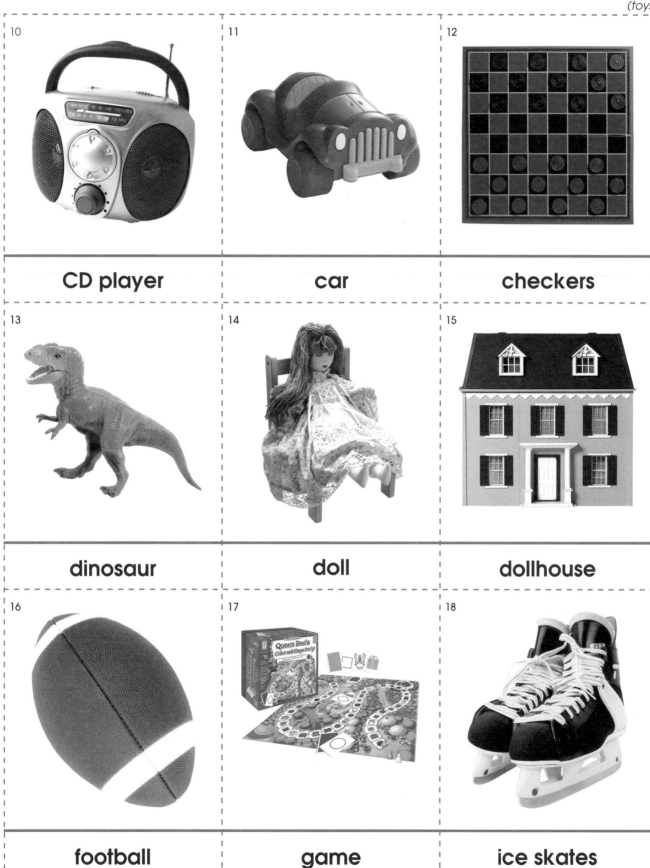

10	11	12
CD player	car	checkers
13	14	15
dinosaur	doll	dollhouse
16	17	18
football	game	ice skates

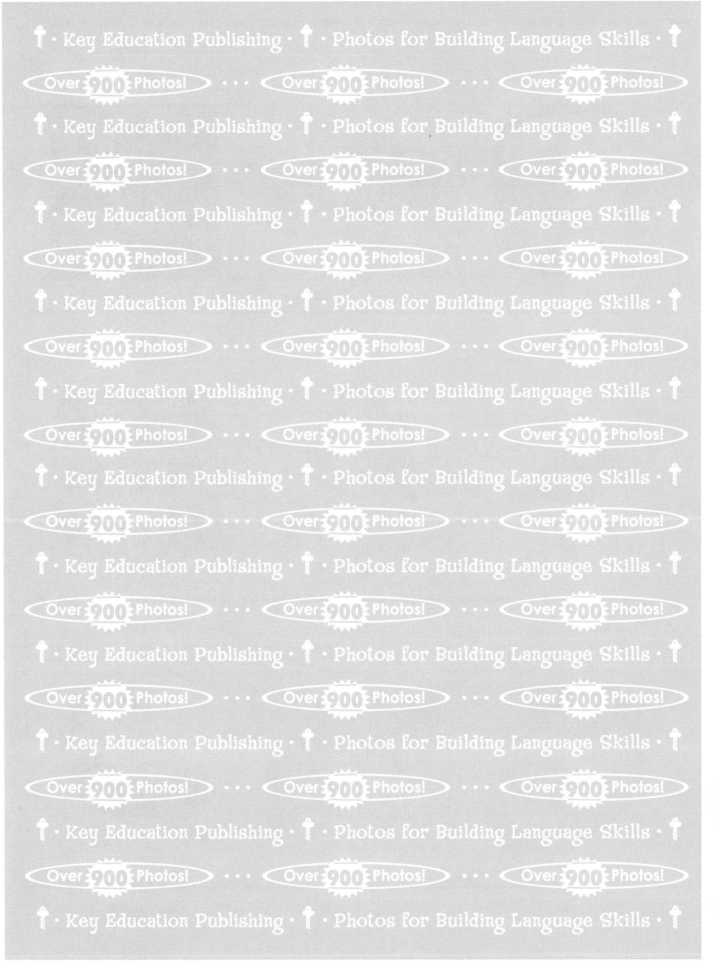

19	20	21
jump rope	kite	magnet
22	23	24
playdough	puzzle	roller blades
25	26	27
rubber ball	sand toys	sled

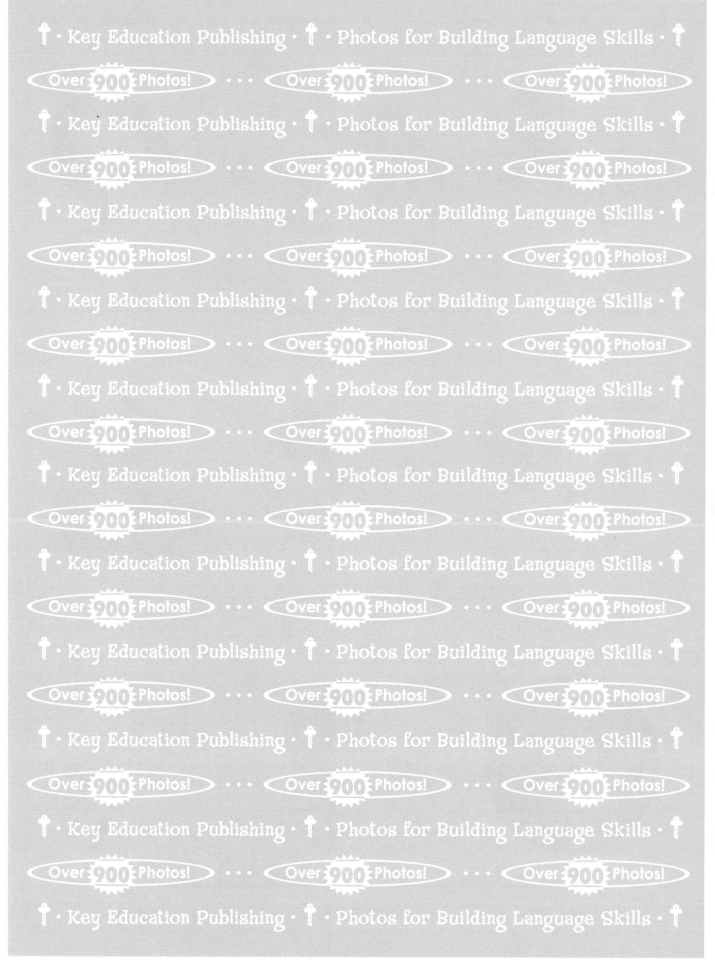

slide	soccer ball	stuffed animal
swing	truck	video game
wagon	wood blocks	yo-yo

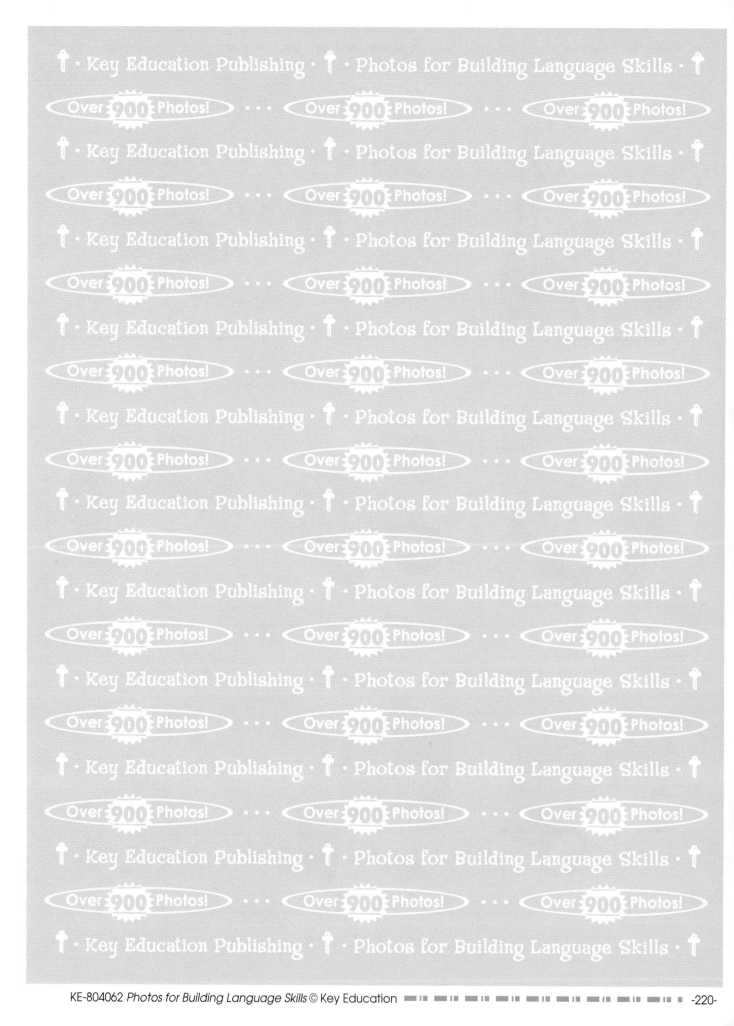

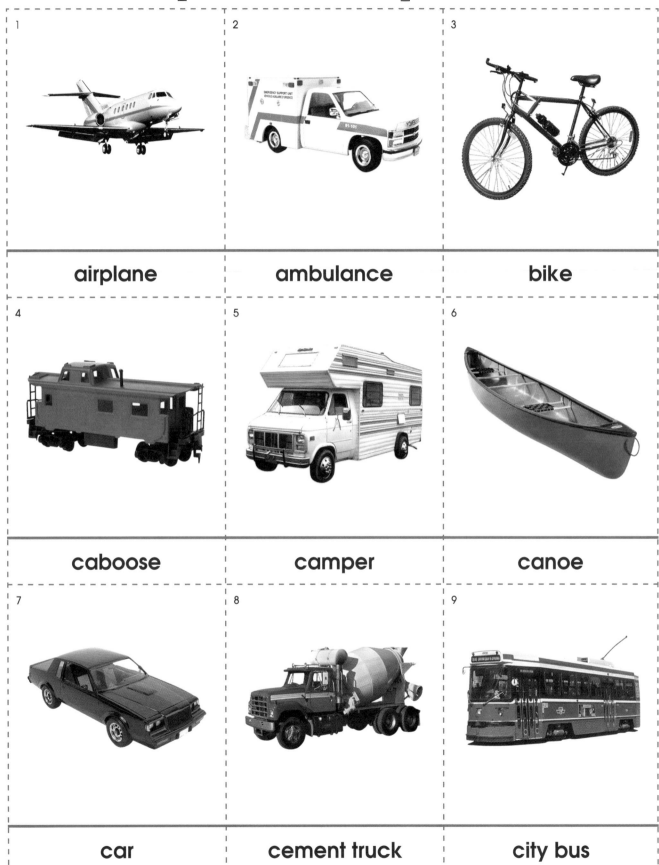

1 airplane	2 ambulance	3 bike
4 caboose	5 camper	6 canoe
7 car	8 cement truck	9 city bus

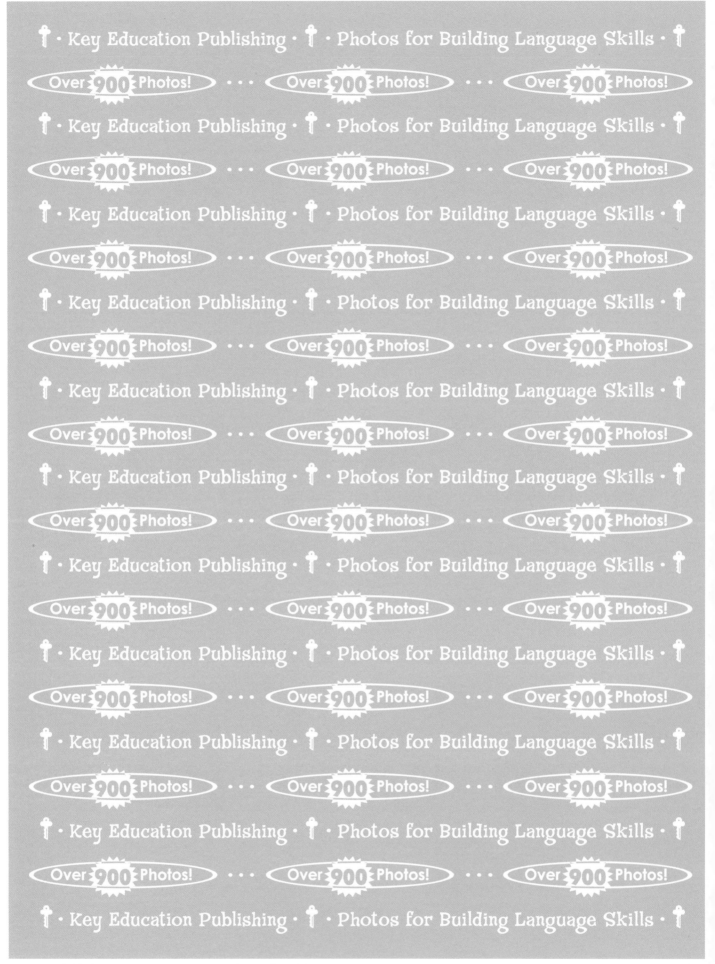

10	11	12
convertible	**diesel truck**	**dump truck**
13	14	15
electric wheelchair	**fire truck**	**helicopter**
16	17	18
hot air balloon	**jeep**	**mini-van**

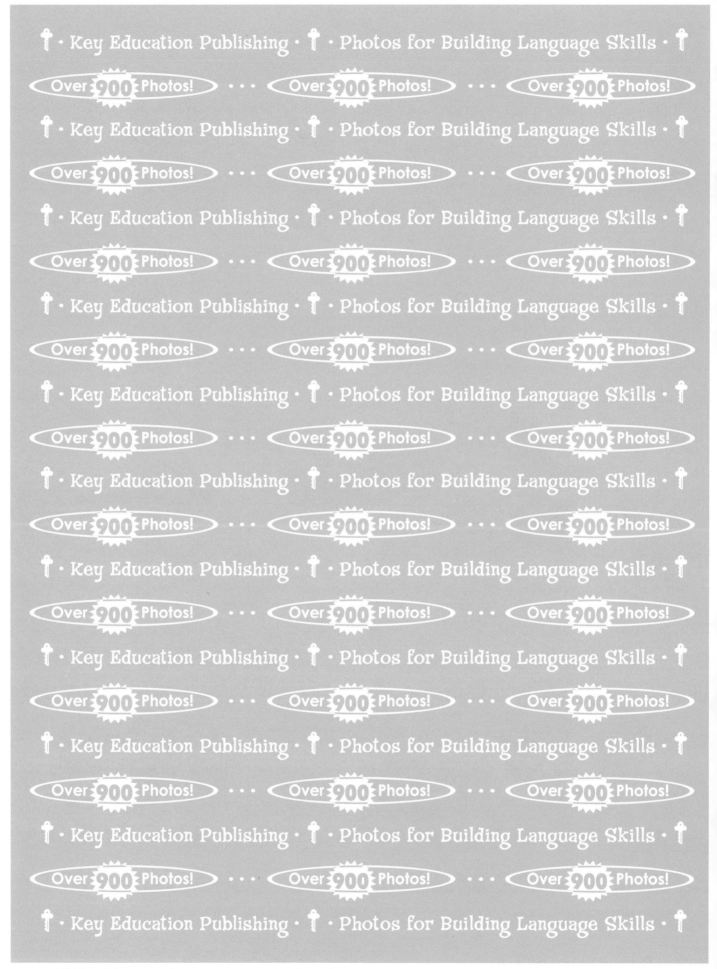

19	20	21
motorcycle	**moving van**	**ocean liner**
22	23	24
pick-up truck	**plow**	**police car**
25	26	27
pontoon boat	**sailboat**	**sanitation truck**

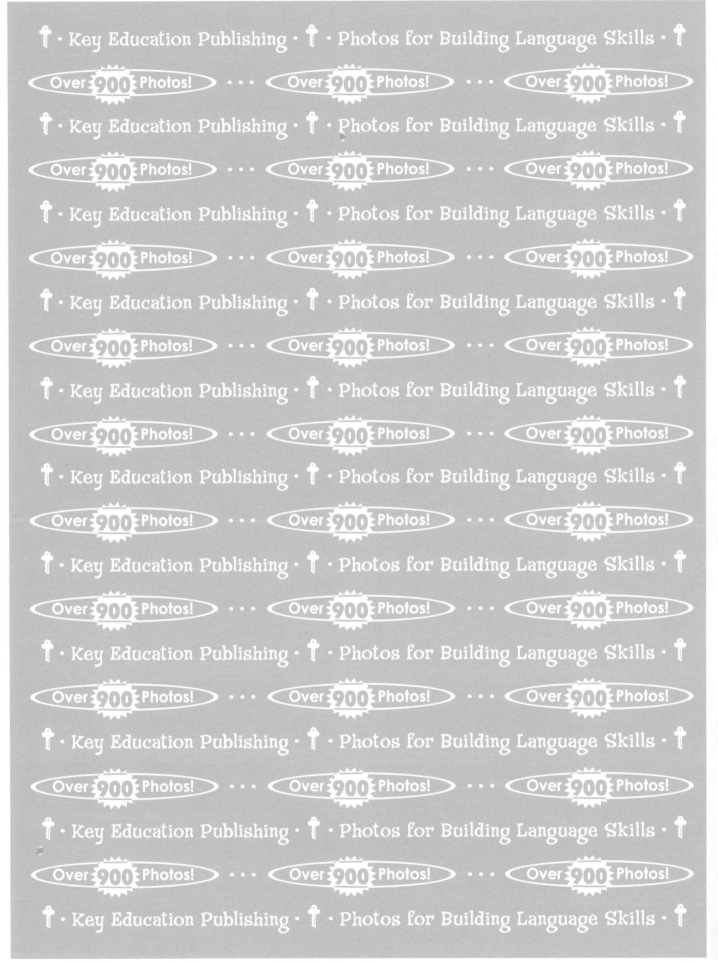

28	29	30
school bus	**ski-doo/jet ski**	**scooter**
31	32	33
skateboard	**snow mobile**	**speed boat**
34	35	36
tow truck	**tractor**	**train**

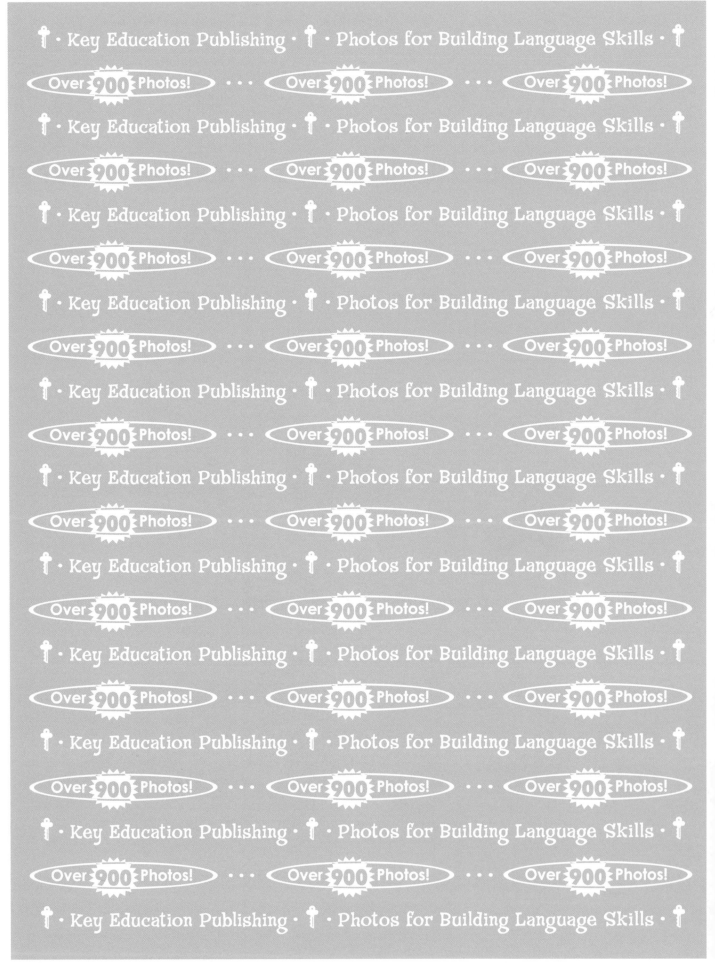

Schedule/Photo Theme: _____

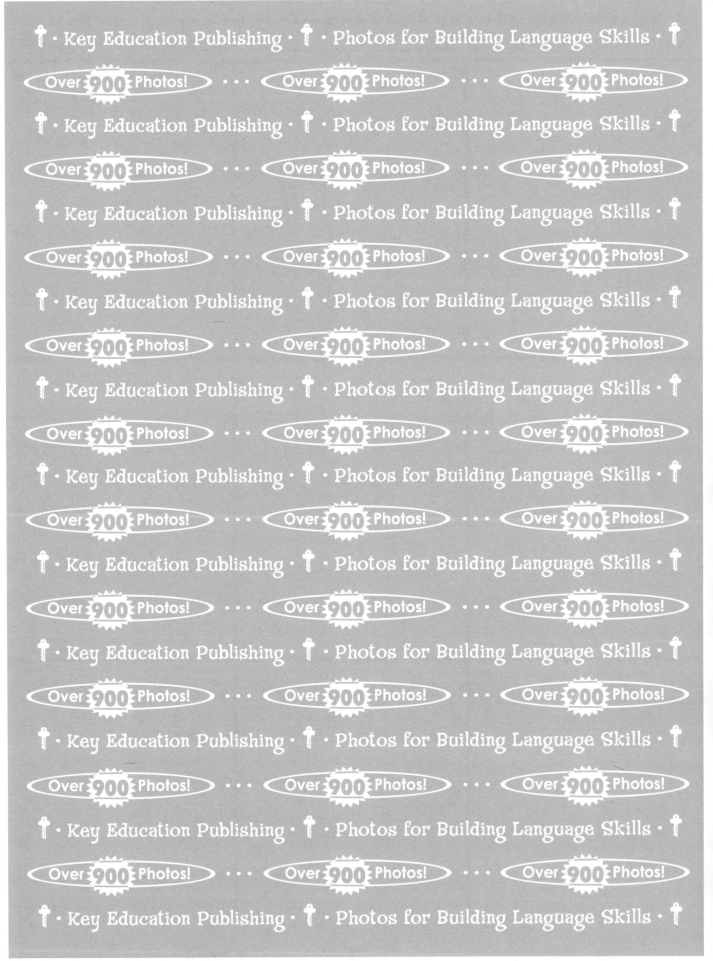

Schedule/Photo Theme: _____

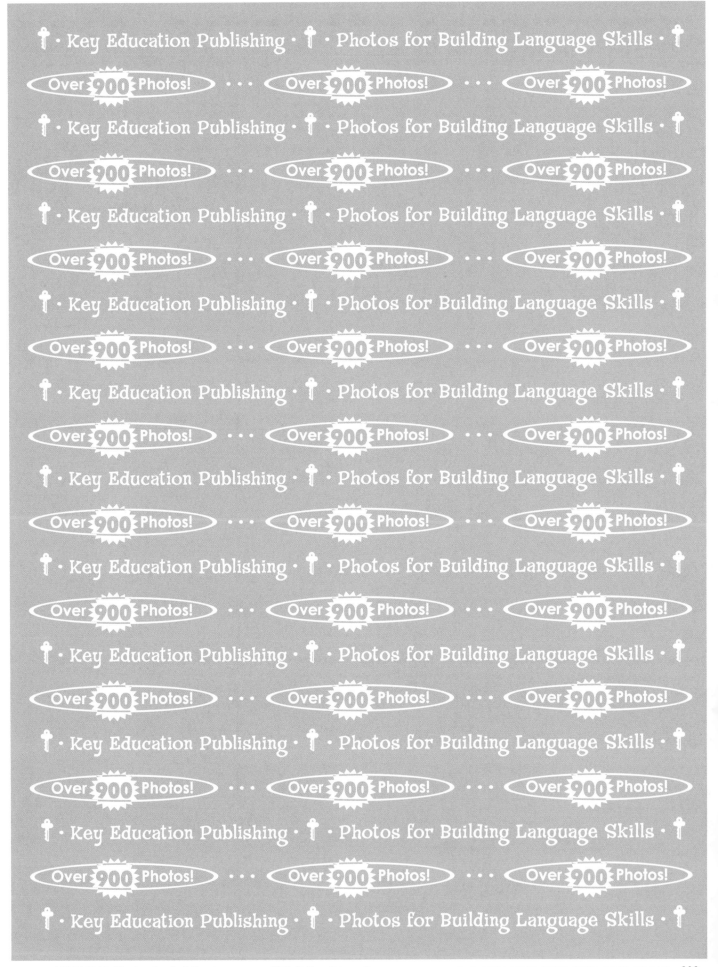

Schedule/Photo Theme: _____

(6-card chart)

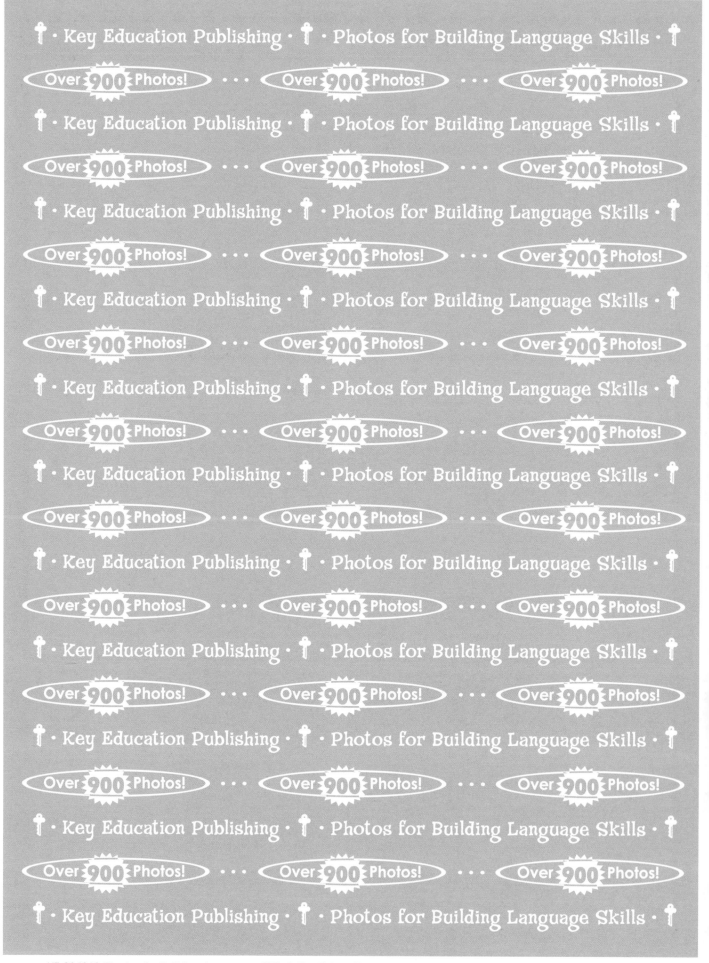

Schedule/Photo Theme: _____

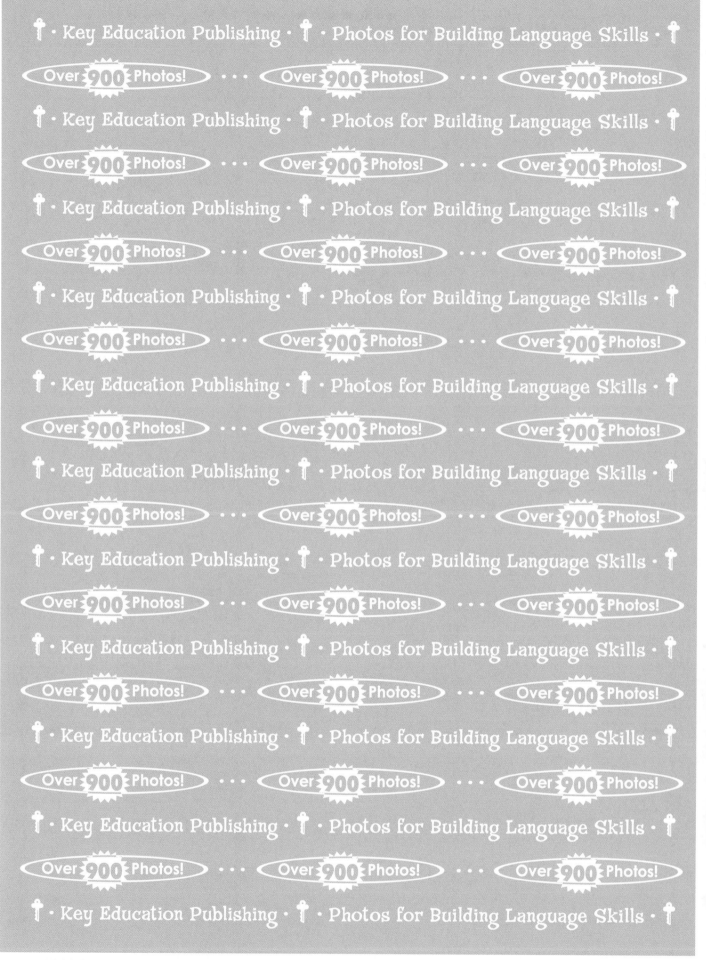

Month _____

Sunday	Monday	Tuesday	Wednesday	Thursday	Friday	Saturday

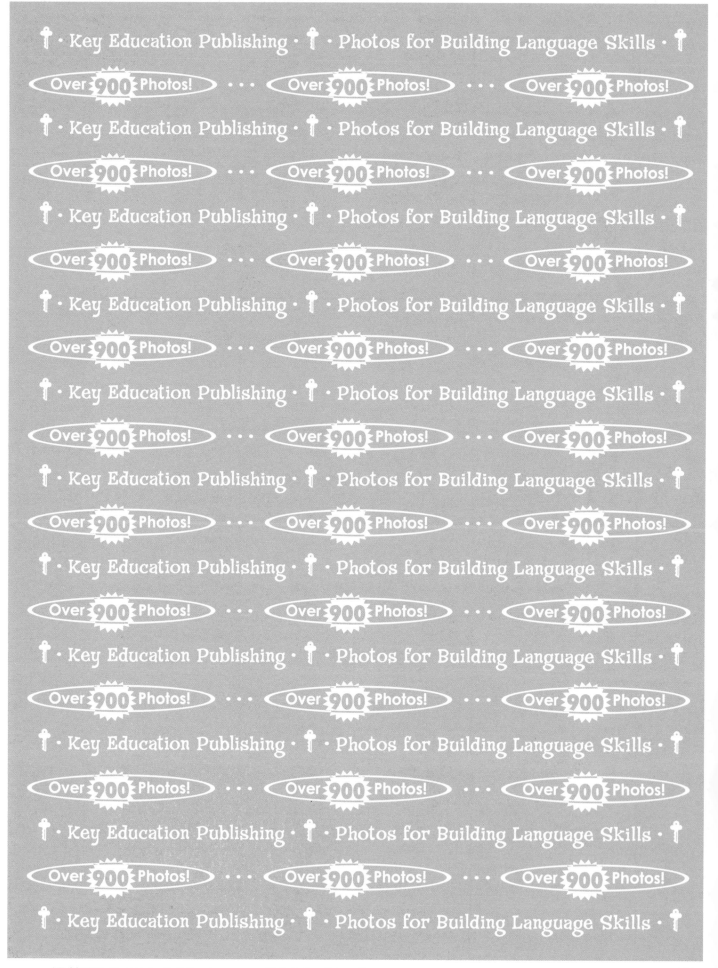

Key Education Publishing Standards Correlation for *Photos for Building Language Skills*

This book supports the NCTE/IRA Standards for the English Language Arts, the recommended teaching practices outlined in the NAEYC/IRA position statement Learning to Read and Write: Developmentally Appropriate Practices for Young Children, the NCTM Principles and Standards for School Mathematics, the National Science Education Standards, and the NCSS Curriculum Standards for Social Studies.

NCTE/IRA Standards for the English Language Arts

Each activity in this book supports one or more of the following standards:

1. **Students read many different types of print and nonprint texts for a variety of purposes.** To use the photographs in *Photos for Building Language Skills*, students learn to read both words and pictures.

2. **Students use a variety of strategies to build meaning while reading.** The activities and photographs in *Photos for Building Language Skills* can be used to develop a variety of reading skills and strategies, including vocabulary, classification, receptive language skills, and sequencing, among others.

3. **Students communicate in spoken, written, and visual form, for a variety of purposes and a variety of audiences.** The photographs in *Photos for Building Language Skills* are specifically designed to be used as a form of visual communication for students with language difficulties. In addition, they help build both spoken and written language skills.

4. **Students use the writing process to write for different purposes and different audiences.** These photographs can be used as story starters or writing prompts for a wide variety of writing projects.

5. **Students whose first language is not English use their first language to learn English and to understand content in all curriculum areas.** *Photos for Building Language Skills* was specifically created for use in English language development programs, enabling ELL students to use their knowledge of their first language to learn vocabulary in English.

6. **Students become participating members of a variety of literacy communities.** The photographs in *Photos for Building Language Skills* can be used as discussion prompts, enabling teachers to build classroom literacy communities.

7. **Students use spoken, written, and visual language for their own purposes such as to learn, for enjoyment, or to share information.** *Photos for Building Language Skills* enables students of many different reading and communication abilities to communicate with others through many different means and for many different reasons.

NAEYC/IRA Position Statement Learning to Read and Write: Developmentally Appropriate Practices for Young Children

Each activity in this book supports one or more of the following recommended teaching practices for preschool students:

1. **Adults create positive relationships with children by talking with them, modeling reading and writing, and building children's interest in reading and writing.** *Photos for Building Language Skills* allows teachers to prompt discussions with their students, building students' interest in reading and writing through the many words and images included in the book.

2. **Teachers provide and draw children's attentions to print-rich learning environments.** The photographs in this book can be used to create a print-rich learning environment.

3. **Teachers provide experiences and materials that help children expand their vocabularies.** *Photos for Building Language Skills* includes hundreds of word and picture cards with accompanying activities that help build students' vocabularies.

Each activity in this book supports one or more of the following recommended teaching practices for kindergarten and primary-grade students:

1. **Teachers provide opportunities for students to write many different kinds of texts for different purposes.** The cards in *Photos for Building Language Skills* can be used as writing prompts for many different kinds of writing projects.

2. **Teachers provide writing experiences that allow children to develop from the use of nonconventional writing forms to more conventional forms.** The cards in *Photos for Building Language Skills* enable students to move from writing and communicating with pictures to writing with words.

3. **Teachers provide challenging instruction that expands children's knowledge of their world and expands their vocabularies.** *Photos for Building Language Skills* includes hundreds of word and picture cards with accompanying activities that help build students' vocabularies.

4. **Teachers adapt teaching strategies based on the individual needs of children.** The many ways to use the cards in *Photos for Building Language Skills* enables teachers to adapt their use to individual children's needs.

This product and the activities in it support the following **Algebra Standard Expectations for Grades Pre-K–2:**
1. **Students sort, classify, and order objects by a variety of properties.** The cards in *Photos for Building Language Skills* can be used in sorting and classification activities that support this standard.

This product and the activities in it support the following **Geometry Standard Expectations for Grades Pre-K–2:**
1. **Students identify, create, draw, compare, and sort two- and three-dimensional shapes.** "Chapter 6: Colors & Shapes" supports this standard.

2. **Students can interpret the relative position of objects.** "Chapter 18: Positional Concepts" supports this standard.

3. **Students describe, name, and interpret direction and distance and use ideas about direction and distance.** "Chapter 18: Positional Concepts" supports this standard.

This product and the activities in it support the following **Measurement Standard Expectations for Grades Pre-K–2:**
1. **Students recognize the characteristics of length, volume, weight, area, and time.** "Chapter 23: Time" supports this standard.

2. **Students compare and order objects according to length, volume, weight, area, and/or time.** "Chapter 23: Time" supports this standard.

3. **Students measure using standard and nonstandard units.** "Chapter 23: Time" supports this standard.

This book and the activities in it support the following **Physical Science Standards for Grades K–4:**
1. **All students should understand the properties of objects and materials.** The photos in "Chapter 15: Opposites" can be used to support this standard.

2. **All students should understand concepts related to the position and motion of objects.** The photos in "Chapter 18: Positional Concepts" can be used to support this standard.

This book and the activities in it support the following **Life Science Standard for Grades K–4:**
1. **All students should understand the characteristics of organisms.** The photos in "Chapter 2: Animals" and "Chapter 4: Body" can be used to support this standard.

This book and the activities in it support the following **Earth and Space Science Standards for Grades K–4:**
1. **All students should understand concepts related to objects in the sky.** The photos in "Chapter 14: Nature & Weather" can be used to support this standard.

2. **All students should understand concepts related to changes in earth and sky.** The photos in "Chapter 10: Holidays & Seasons" and "Chapter 14: Nature & Weather" can be used to support this standard.

This book and the activities in it support the following **Science and Technology Standard for Grades K–4:**
1. **All students should develop the ability to distinguish natural objects from human-made objects.** Because they include many natural and human-made objects, many of the photographs throughout *Photos for Building Language Skills* can be used to support this standard.

The activities in this book support the following performance expectations for students in the early grades: **People, Places, and Environment**
1. **Students can describe and make predictions about changes to physical systems, like seasons, climate, weather, and the water cycle.** The photos in "Chapter 14: Nature & Weather" can be used to support this standard.

The activities in this book support the following performance expectations for students in the early grades: **Individual Development and Identity**
1. **Students describe things that make their families unique.** The photos in "Chapter 16: People & Family" can be used to support this standard.

The activities in this book support the following performance expectations for students in the early grades: **Production, Distribution, and Consumption**
1. **Students describe how workers with specific jobs contribute to the production and trade of goods and services.** Photos in "Chapter 16: People & Family" can be used to support this standard.